AN ODE TO FRATERNITY

AN ODE TO FRATERNITY

Life, Death &
Beyond in
World Religion
....
Is There Unity
in Diversity?

ROHINTON
F. NARIMAN

VINTAGE
An imprint of Penguin Random House

VINTAGE

Vintage is an imprint of the Penguin Random House group of companies
whose addresses can be found at global.penguinrandomhouse.com

Published by Penguin Random House India Pvt. Ltd
4th Floor, Capital Tower 1, MG Road,
Gurugram 122 002, Haryana, India

Penguin
Random House
India

First published in Vintage by Penguin Random House India 2025

ISBN 9780143472001

Typeset in EB Garamond by MAP Systems, Bengaluru, India
Printed at Replika Press Pvt. Ltd, India

www.penguin.co.in

MIX
Paper | Supporting
responsible forestry
FSC™ C016779

This book is built on optimism and hope. It is a small but vital step towards world peace that can only endure if mankind can learn to live with its differences and can learn to settle them through understanding, dialogue and non-violence

Contents

Part III: Hinduism

Part IV

Part V

THE DALAI LAMA

FOREWORD

One of my four main commitments in life is the promotion of religious harmony. As a spiritual practitioner, I feel religions exist to serve humanity. Although there are philosophical differences between world's major religious traditions, all of them adhere to the practice of compassion and a sense of responsibility. As human beings are diverse, with different social and spiritual upbringings as well as intellectual capabilities, there are diverse religious traditions to meet different needs, just as we have different medical systems, each with their own way of treating an affliction.

In the course of my life, interacting with many religious leaders as well as people of different faiths has helped me appreciate this common element that binds us all together. This experience has instilled in me a great sense of fulfilment and an assurance of our shared humanity. While we may differ philosophically, the purpose of our religions is to create happiness in our life. Therefore, respecting the faith of others and nurturing a sense of appreciation for their teachings is very beneficial. In our ever more interconnected world, it is increasingly important to treat every faith tradition with humility and respect.

I commend Rohinton Nariman for writing this book *An Ode to Fraternity*, which gives an overview of the major religious traditions. I hope readers may find it useful when it comes to understanding the essence of different religions, even as they remain faithful to their own tradition.

20 November 2024

Oswald Cardinal Gracias

RCHBISHOP'S HOUSE
21, Nathalal Parekh Marg,
Mumbai 400 001. Fax: 91-22-2285 3872
Tel: 2202 1093, 2202 1193, 2202 1293
Email: diocesebombay@gmail.com

Foreword

In a world where division often seems louder than unity, where conflicts persist in regions that have known little peace for generations, it is rare for a voice to rise that calls us to pause, reflect, and reconsider our shared humanity. Justice Nariman's *An Ode to Fraternity: Life, Death and Beyond in World Religions – Is There Unity in Diversity?* offers such a voice. With eloquence, wisdom, and a deep sense of moral responsibility, Justice Nariman challenges us to look beyond the fractures that separate us and to recognize the profound unity that lies at the heart of all human endeavors, especially as reflected through the teachings of the world's great religious traditions.

In a career marked by distinguished service on India's Supreme Court, Justice Nariman has become a trusted arbiter of justice, balancing legal rigor with ethical insight. In this book, he turns his attention from the courtroom to the broader realm of human relationships, seeking to understand and promote the values that have always united rather than divided us: fraternity, compassion, and respect for the dignity of others.

Justice Nariman's inquiry is not merely academic. The current global landscape, with its seemingly unending conflicts and humanitarian crises, serves as the backdrop for this book's earnest question: How can we, despite our differences, recognize our shared humanity? This is a question not just for individuals, but for societies, for cultures, for nations. And Justice Nariman approaches it with a humility that draws on his own personal experience and his deep respect for the ethical teachings of the world's religions.

One of the book's most important messages is the recognition that, while religions may differ in their metaphysical outlooks, they are united in their ethical foundations. Across all faiths, there runs a common thread—the belief that how we live our lives, the choices we make, and the way we treat one another carries profound moral consequences. *An Ode to Fraternity* challenges us to examine our own beliefs and actions, urging us not to become mired in dogmatic divisions but to see, instead, the universal principles that encourage kindness, peace, and respect for others.

At a time when religious intolerance, ideological rigidity, and the abuse of power seem to shape much of the global discourse, Justice Nariman's book stands as a hopeful counterpoint. It is a timely call for a deeper understanding of each other's differences, a plea for mutual respect, and a vision of a world where fraternity is not just a lofty ideal but a lived reality. The insights into the dangers of fanaticism and the misuse of religious teachings remind us that true spirituality is always accompanied by a profound sense of responsibility to the other—a recognition that the welfare of one is inextricably linked to the welfare of all.

In the pages that follow, we are invited to reflect on the ethical commonalities that transcend the particularities of any single tradition, to consider how the pursuit of peace can be better realized through dialogue, mutual respect, and shared moral purpose. Justice Nariman's dream of a world that transcends violence and embraces the principle of fraternity is not a utopian fantasy, but a realistic goal—one that requires collective effort, compassion, and a recognition of our common humanity. May this book inspire all of us to look beyond the divisions of the present and move toward a future where, in the words of Schiller, we truly recognize that "all men are brothers."

+ *Osw E Gracias*

+Oswald Cardinal Gracias
Archbishop of Bombay

January 14, 2025

Preface

Life, Death and Beyond in World Religions: Is There Unity in Diversity?

This book is an attempt to remind the human race that we are all brothers and sisters, and that we should live in peace and harmony. Two world wars are not enough to bring the human race to its senses. As I write this book, two theatres of war are ongoing: one in Gaza and the other in Ukraine. It does seem that we are ordained to fight and kill each other instead of loving one another and giving the respect due to another's point of view. Instead of 'live and let live', the motto today seems to be 'live and let the other die'. Brotherhood and Sisterhood seem to be utopian—a mere chimera. Ludwig van Beethoven, one of the greatest composers that ever lived, after struggling for what he thought was missing in his final ninth symphony, laid his hands on the most famous German poet Schiller's 'Ode to Joy'. He had it sung in the last movement of this celebrated composition. Schiller's message was simple: All men are brothers, who custom has divided.

It is important not to stop here but to move on and find some solution to this seemingly intractable problem. The way was shown by Emperor Ashoka over 2000 years ago in his twelfth major rock edict. In it, he proclaimed to the world that he honoured all sects and considered the advancement of the 'essential doctrine' of all sects to be most important. Its basis is the control of one's speech so as not to extol one's own sect while disparaging another's. On every occasion, one should honour another person's sect, for by doing so, one increases the influence of one's own sect and benefits from that of the other's. While by doing otherwise, one diminishes the influence of one's own sect and harms the other's. In other words, whoever honours his own sect or disparages that of another, harms his own sect. Therefore, concord is to be commended, so that men may hear each other's principles and respect them. This is the desire of the emperor, that all sects should be well informed and should teach that which is good and that everywhere their adherents should be told this. The emperor does not consider gifts or honours to be as important as the progress of the essential doctrine of all sects. And the result is the increased influence of one's own sect and glory to dharma.

The great saint Ramakrishna Paramahansa showed mankind the way by following both Christianity and Islam. Later, he declared that he reached the same Godhead through these faiths as he reached through his devotion to the Mother Goddess.

Fanatics are the same worldwide, although their labels may be different. They also have the same characteristics. They do not really understand the religion to which they belong and they do not want to understand the religion of other people. Their favourite ploy is to pick up and tear a particular passage from a holy text out of its context so as to denigrate another's religion.

This book will, hopefully, pass on the message that though the religions of the world may differ in their metaphysical content, the ethical basis of all of them remains similar. That every good deed produces happiness and that, conversely, every evil deed recoils on the perpetrator. 'As you sow so shall you reap' is the message that we get through all world religions. In essence, they preach that the means to reach the end advocated by them must be pure and noble. And this purity and nobility must also translate itself into being good to mankind as a whole. We must never forget that the greatest mass murderers in history are those who do not believe in what the world's great religions teach. They believe only in power. As Baron Acton's famous letter to Archbishop Creighton showed: 'Power tends to corrupt and absolute power corrupts absolutely.' It is not an accident that Mao Tse-tung and Stalin are the greatest mass murderers in history. Neither of them had any concept of what the world's religions teach—that every evil action begets an equal and opposite reaction which recoils on the perpetrator.

My dream is that at some point, sooner rather than later, the utopia of world peace no longer remains utopian. And I do hope that we do not have to first destroy ourselves in order to discover that non-violence and fraternity alone can make humanity reach this goal.

Part I: The Monotheistic Faiths

Zoroastrianism

Zarathustra is appointed by Almighty God as the first person to ever receive a revelation from one God. Zarathustra himself belonged to a period of Persian history which antedated the Achaemenian dynasty (550–330 BCE), the founder of which was King Cyrus the Great. The epic poem 'Shahnamah', written by Firdausi, tells us that there were two dynasties before the third great Persian dynasty of King Cyrus the Great, namely, the Peshdadanian and the Kayanian. Prophet Zarathustra belonged to the period of the latter dynasty. He converted King Vistasp to his new faith, resulting in a mass conversion of the King's subjects. The age of the Prophet is indeterminate, varying from as much as 6500–1000 BCE.

What was revealed to Zarathustra has come down to us in the form of 238 hymns, which are collectively referred to as the *Gatha*s. What these hymns tell us is that the Prophet belonged to the old Rigvedic religion until he received a revelation from one Creator God. This great God replaced the deva worship (the worship of many gods) of the Rigveda, which essentially consisted of worshipping nature deities. Zarathustra states in unmistakable terms that there is only one God, and names him Ahura Mazda, meaning the Lord who is the great Creator.

It is important to first state what the two basic prayers in Zoroatrianism mean—the 'Ashem Vohu' prayer and the 'Yatha Ahu Vairyo' prayer. The 'Ashem Vohu' prayer concerns itself with two concepts, truth and happiness, forging a causal link between the two. It goes thus:

> Truth is good, Indeed it is best. It is happiness.
> Happiness comes to him, who, for the sake of truth, follows the path of truth.

The 'Yatha Ahu Vairyo' prayer is in three parts. Part one is a reaffirmation of the 'Ashem Vohu' prayer, emphasizing the fact that it is the truthful who ultimately triumph, not the powerful. It says:

> Just as a Great Lord (on Earth) is very powerful, so is a teacher (who is spiritual), for the reason that he lives by the path of truth.

The second part of the prayer speaks of the highest gifts that can be bestowed on a human mind, which will be so given only if good deeds are done in this life, for the love of the great Creator. And the third part gives Zoroastrians a sense of charity. It states that he who helps any person in need will, in turn, be helped through the power of Almighty God.

Ahura Mazda is said to be the worthiest being that can be invoked in prayer. He is slow to anger but should never be provoked to wrath. He is all-pervasive, being the Creator of everything that exists. He is the father of all the great ideals of truth, the good mind, and right-mindedness. He is the judge over all the actions of the living. Nothing escapes Him as He is all-seeing and can never be deceived. He is all-powerful and exists entirely by Himself, having no second or equal. He dwells in various worlds described as worlds of truth or reality, and stands as the ultimate goal to which all creation advances. He has fashioned this Earth to give joy to mankind, in His wisdom. He is truth-tongued and is the teacher of mankind, from the very beginning, through Vohu Manah (the Pure or Good Mind). He is to be worshipped, not out of fear but out of love and friendship.

We are told that God appointed Zarathustra as a teacher for all mankind to tell them of the path of truth and how to live in accordance with the truth. In a specific verse of great poignancy in the *Gathas*, he shows his humility by asking the Almighty to take pity on him when he is judged. The mode of revelation of the new faith is pointed out in some of these verses, which is the Pure Mind entering Zarathustra and telling him what he should tell mankind. In an interesting verse, he lays down two important principles: one, to fight evil to the extent that one is capable of so doing, and second, to pray to Fire being the physical embodiment of a spiritual being, namely Truth. In perhaps the most important verse in the *Gathas* (Zarathustra's hymns), Chapter 45, Verse 8, Prophet Zarathustra finally gets to perceive God himself with his mind's eye, pursuant to which the Holy Trinity of good thoughts, good words and good deeds is laid down as the path of Truth which mankind is to

follow. The last two verses of the last *Gatha* state how Prophet
Zarathustra's mission was successful. He conquered death and
was granted life for all eternity.

Asha or truth is the backbone of Zoroastrianism. Truth is
so important that it occurs in almost every verse of the *Gatha*s.
Absolute Truth and relative Truth are described by the same
word, the context telling us whether it is the former or the
latter. *Yasna* 29.3, the religious compilation in which the
Gathas occur, mentions two interesting attributes of absolute
Truth: First, that it does not disunite, i.e., it is the ultimate
moral binding force of all mankind, and second, that like the
sun which shines on good and evil alike, it is inimical to none.

Vohu Manah, which literally means the good mind, is
almost as important as Asha, and recurs throughout the
*Gatha*s. It is through Vohu Manah that God's revelations
are made known to Zarathustra. Since life on Earth, and
in the hereafter, has to do with the mind/spirit, it is Vohu
Manah whose gifts are most precious. The basic 'Yatha Ahu
Vairyo' prayer, in its second part, speaks of these gifts. These
gifts are set out in *Yasna* 45.10, and are four in number:

Tevishi: that is strength of character
Utayuiti: life renewed or taking on a different
direction or course
Hu Urva Tat: wholeness or perfection
Amere Tat: immortality

The first two gifts are given to a human being here on Earth
and are the by-products of following the path of Truth. The

last two gifts are given to mankind only after it has been completely cleansed of evil and are therefore only bestowed in the hereafter.

Spenta Mainyu, literally translated, refers to the holy or good spirit. This holy spirit was created at the beginning of time and was given the choice of whether it would be beneficent or malignant. It chose the former. Interestingly enough, its twin, which is its equal in every respect, was also given the same choice, but it chose to be malignant. Angra Mainyu, or the evil spirit, is all that exists as the embodiment of evil in the *Gathas*. There is no devil here who is both powerful and an opposing force to Almighty God. God is clearly omnipotent in the *Gathas*, and evil is only equated with wrong moral choice.

Gatha verses refer to the holy spirit, Spenta Mainyu, in some detail. In these verses, Zarathustra chooses to be like Spenta Mainyu, who is equated with the highest moral state that any human mind can achieve. This spirit speaks in accordance with the Pure Mind's revelations and fulfils the tasks that any right-minded person must do, inspired by the fact that God alone is the Father of Truth. Importantly, it is on account of this spirit that evil people feel thwarted and righteous persons feel comforted. Spenta Mainyu is clearly the spirit which, when it works in man's brain, produces results which are in accordance with the teachings of the Pure Mind.

Sarosh, or conscience, or the moral voice that speaks from within, is described as the greatest of all the attributes of mankind. This is so because it is only by hearing this inner voice that the path of truth can be followed in obedience to God's law. There is also an enigmatic verse in the *Gathas* which says that Sarosh is so powerful that it can even hear hymns sung by devotees in heaven.

Armaiti, right-mindedness or faith, is said to grow through the teachings or revelations of the Pure Mind. It is the human beings' guide; it stands by whenever there is doubt, to resolve it in moral terms. She is said to withdraw from persons who make the wrong moral choice. She alone imparts real understanding of the path of Truth, being the root of this eternal law. The devotee of Armaiti is stated to be wise. And wisdom is defined as those teachings and actions which go together to promote Truth.

Two whole chapters of the *Gatha*s are dedicated to sermons addressed by Prophet Zarathustra to the multitude. The lesser sermon, so named because it is a sermon only to his own people, is contained in Chapter 30, which is the third chapter of the first or *Ahunavaiti Gatha*. The greater sermon, that is addressed to persons who have come from both nearby and from afar, is contained in Chapter 45, which is the third chapter of the second or *Ustavaiti Gatha*. Both sermons deliver the central message of the *Gatha*s and must therefore be understood fully as well as correctly.

Chapter 30 begins by saying that every person must decide for himself as to what moral choice he or she is to make so that life's onward journey is either towards light and happiness or towards darkness and misery. The sermon begins by speaking of the twin spirits created by God at the beginning of time. They were equal in every respect except that one spirit chose to be good in thought, word and deed, whereas its twin chose to be evil. Together, they created life and its destruction so that Creation's purpose may be fulfilled: the best for the followers of truth and the worst for the followers of evil. Those who believed in the old faith—those who believed in many gods— have deluded themselves and polluted life through anger and hatred born of evil thoughts. The path of Truth, on which people continually progress, is likened to going through molten metal. God's law is revealed to all sinners only when retribution comes to them for their sins, at which point they actually achieve their real, innermost desire, i.e., to be one with God and His archangels. The sermon ends by stating that moral choice leads either to happiness or to misery, which is either upward progress towards illumination and hence happiness, or age-long punishment for sins committed and hence misery.

The greater sermon contained in Chapter 45 is in some ways an emphatic reiteration of the smaller sermon, but with greater intensity. It begins with a reiteration of the theme of the twin spirits and states how they are exactly opposite in every possible respect. The twin concepts of 'Hu Urva Tat' and 'Amere Tat' are then spoken about. 'Hu Urva Tat' is nothing more and nothing less than a state of being by which each soul is 'Hu', which is good, whole or perfect, and rid of all evil. When this state of being occurs, 'Amere Tat' also takes place, which is that such a soul will be in a state where death is permanently removed.

The Prophet then goes on to say that the soul of the righteous becomes immortal, but ever renewed are troubles and tribulations to the evil soul. Verse 8 in Chapter 45 is arguably the single most important verse in the entire *Gatha*s, for it is here that Zarathustra, having seen God with his mind's eye, lays down the Holy Trinity of good thoughts, good words and good deeds, and goes on to say that anybody who follows these three will surely land up in heaven, which is described by two words: 'Garo Deman'. Interestingly, both words are words in common usage today—the first in the Gujarati language, and the second in English itself. This is because Avestan is an old language belonging to the Indo-European group of languages, of which Gujarati and English are younger languages. 'Ga' in Gujarati means 'song', which is the same in Hindi: 'gaana'. 'Deman' is the English 'domain', which leads to heaven being described as the 'domain' or abode of song. 'Tevishi' means 'strength of character', and 'Utayuiti' means 'life renewed'. When one follows the path of truth, one finds that it is a path filled with difficulties. When these difficulties are overcome, two things are assured: first, strength of character, as that alone has enabled the person to overcome these difficulties, and second, that life takes on a new meaning and direction. While earlier, one may have been cowardly and greedy, one becomes strong and giving after overcoming difficulties. It is with these two gifts and the two concepts of 'Hu Urva Tat' and 'Amere Tat' that this magnificent sermon ends, giving the listener great hope and instructing her/ him about what happens when the path of Truth is followed, both here in life and after death.

Apart from what is stated in the two great sermons, there are verses of the *Gatha*s that further explain the moral teachings of Zarathustra. These verses stress the fact that human beings have been created not as puppets but as thinking beings, capable of moral choices. Human beings are apart from animal creation in this respect, and perhaps the worship of fire as a symbol of truth or correct moral choice is also because (apart from fire being light) an animal cannot light, kindle or put out a fire. It is, therefore, the symbol of moral choice par excellence. So, a human being, by using his conscience, can light as well as kindle his inner fire and, by ceasing to use his conscience, puts the same fire out. Chapter 34, Verse 13, restates the teaching of every great saviour. It is that every good deed inspired by truth alone reaches far. Likewise, Verse 5 of Chapter 43 makes it clear that all acts and words bear fruit; nobody can escape the consequences of their acts and words. Another interesting verse—Chapter 46, Verse 6—makes the dichotomy between good and evil crystal clear by declaring that he who is good to those who are evil is himself evil, and he who is good to the righteous is himself righteous.

These verses also tell us that it is through striving by one's own inner urge and self-sacrifice that one understands and then follows revelatory truths; ultimately, the highest is reached and the laws of God are followed only through good deeds.

Zarathustra was a staunch follower of monotheism. The followers of the old religion, who believe in many gods, are described as angry and, therefore, harmful to those who lead a moral life. They are said to be of the false spirit—they are liars who are self-centred, and indulge in doublespeak. They have strayed from the path of Truth. Yet, they are an extremely powerful group, and men doing the worst deeds are said to be the beloveds of the gods, spreading hatred and making mankind wail in bondage.

Three such persons are singled out by name. The first is Yima, who is none other than the famous King Jamshed after whom the Navroz festival, observed on the 21st March of every year, is named. He is said to have illumined the material side of the Earth instead of the spiritual, and is thus condemned by Zarathustra. The other person mentioned by name is Grehma, who may well have been some evil priest or king. He is said to doom life to death, but once reformed by suffering, will ask to be instructed correctly so that he may also be whole or without evil. The third person named is Bendva, who is said to be both a liar and duplicitous by nature. This led Zarathustra to forbid his flock from associating with such persons in general.

Two verses are of particular interest, one dealing with black magic, and the other with the Soma cult. In Chapter 32.10, we are told about a group of black magicians who say that seeing the Earth and the Sun are bad as both will interfere with their nefarious deeds. Another interesting verse is in Chapter 48.10, which seems to refer to the Rigvedic cult of Soma. Soma is said to be the juice which intoxicates the gods in the Rigveda. Apparently, this cult seems to have been powerful in Zarathustra's time and was denounced by him, stating that the priests of this cult falsely fascinated persons with 'muther', the same as the Gujarati word for 'urine'. The extremes of drug and alcohol abuse are what the Prophet is railing against here. These verses further go on to tell us not to be taken in by worldly grandeur and alluring speech. False preachers are said to distort the scriptures and separate us from our real heritage. Their deeds and teachings show them for who they really are. Ultimately, such persons are described as persons of poor understanding, for if they understood and knew that every evil action will have its recompense in the other world, and hence recoil on the evil person himself, they would not continue to be evil.

Zarathustra repeatedly questioned God as to what punishment was in store for evil persons, here on Earth. His answer was that retribution occurs at death, and that every soul will judge for itself where it is to go, depending on how it has lived life on Earth. After death, the soul goes down the bridge of the separator and based on its thoughts, words and deeds, it consigns itself to either heaven, which is the abode of song, or hell, which is the abode of miserable existence. In heaven, the soul enjoys happiness and light, whereas in hell it is given retribution for its evil deeds by God Himself, which is described as an age-long punishment in darkness.

The idea of such retribution, however, is so that God's laws can be revealed to those who have not followed them on Earth, the idea being that even at a later stage, they are given a chance to make the correct moral choice. A cut-off date or Judgement Day will arrive after which all souls will triumph in Hu Urva Tat and Amere Tat (perfection of character coupled with immortality), which is none other than the ultimate resurrection that is to take place on Earth.

The verses on prayer divide themselves into three groups. The first speaks of prayer being important as a reminder of how to lead life morally. The second makes it clear that, correctly stated, prayers will guide the path of a person's tongue, so that she/ he may both instruct other persons and lift up her/ his voice in adoration of God. The third verse tells us that if something is asked for by way of prayer, it is answered, provided that what is asked for is righteous. We are told that the best reward that prayer can give is goodness, as it enures the benefit of everybody. Some of the verses tell us how both—persons who are good as well as persons who are evil—pray, so that unless prayer is directed to righteous ends, it is of no avail. The verses in Chapter 50 speak of ecstatic singing of hymns which brings mankind back to its Creator. 'Happiness to him who gives happiness to whomsoever else' is the opening statement of the Ustavaiti or second *Gatha*. What is achieved by following the path of truth is happiness here on Earth and upward progress in the realms of light hereafter. One other interesting thing spoken of is the fact that light arises from within and it is from striving for light that man ultimately attains light.

Yasnahaptangaiti

The Yasnahaptangaiti, one of the oldest Aryan texts, is contained in seven chapters, the chapters being 'Yasna'

35–41 of the compilation which is called the 'Yajashne', consisting of seventy-two chapters. This Yasna or worship is sandwiched between the first two *Gatha*s. The hymns appear to be composed after Zarathustra's death, and are in prose not poetry. There is a distinct shift in this Yasna as several major nature deities of the Rigveda come back in it but in Zoroastrianised form. Thus, there is praise to Ahura Mazda and the Holy Immortals who we have already encountered in the *Gatha*s. There is then praise to Ahura and the fire, the sacred waters, etc. After the Yasnahaptangaiti come the 'Yashts' which are hymns of praise in Avesta to various lesser beings who are accommodated as angels.

In the Yashts, we find a polytheism which is very similar to that of the great hymn-cycle of the earliest Indo-Aryans— the Rigveda—a polytheism against which Zoroaster, the Iranian religious reformer, rebelled. Both in the Yashts and in the Rigveda, we have a plurality of gods, and they have similar names in both the texts. Thus, in the Rigveda, we meet with Mitra, Aryaman, Vayu, Dhata and Yama, and in the Yashts we have Mithra, Airyaman, Vayu, Dhata and Yima. These gods succeeded in re-establishing themselves after the Zoroastrian reform, and in the Yashts they become angels. However, by way of contrast, we find entities which are important gods in the Rigveda, but which appear as demons in the Avesta: the principal among these being Indra, Sarva (Saurva) and Nasatya (Nanghaithya). This was the direct result of the Zoroastrian reform, for all these gods are called Deva in the Vedas, and they retain this name (Daeva) in the Avesta. However, for

Zarathustra and his successors, this term means not 'God' but 'demon'.

Thus the Zoroastrian reform demonised that class of deity which was called Deva and eliminated the other class of deity called Ahura by the Iranians and Asura by the Indians, with the single exception of Ahura Mazda (later called Ohrmazd) who was elevated to the status of the one true God from whom all other divinities proceeded. Against this God was Angra Mainyu (Ahriman), the Destructive Spirit. Life on earth is represented as a battle between Spenta Mainyu, the holy spirit, on the one hand, and Angra Mainyu and his demonic hordes, on the other. For Zarathustra, it was a very real battle since the worshippers of the devas were still the representatives of the old religion. Among their practices, one was an animal sacrifice in which a bull was the victim; Zarathustra was against it. In the Yashts, too, we find repeated references to animal sacrifice.

It is only in the Pahlavi texts in the Sasanian period (224–651 CE) that we find a return to the spirit of the *Gathas*. The old Ahura Mazda, who is now called Ohrmazd, is the principle of good, and Ahriman (Angra Mainyu) is the principle of evil. The Amesha Spentas or 'Bounteous Immortals' and the Yazatas or the angels are below the One Creator God. Similarly, in his own realm, Ahriman is all powerful and the other demons are his creations. The text below is from the Pahlavi scriptures and is set out in full as it instructs every person who reaches the age of maturity (fifteen years, in Persia) about the essentials of the Zoroastrian religion, which he/she is about to join.

Select Counsels of the Ancient Sages

(1)   In conformity with the revelation of the Religion the ancient sages, in their primeval wisdom, have said that on reaching the age of fifteen every man and woman must know the answer to these questions: 'Who am I? To whom do I belong? From whence have I come? and whither do I return? From what stock and lineage am I? What is my function and duty on earth? and what is my reward in the world to come? Did I come forth from the unseen world? or was I (always) of this world? Do I belong to Ohrmazd or to Ahriman? Do I belong to the gods or to the demons? Do I belong to the good or to the wicked? Am I a man or a demon? How many paths are there (to salvation)? What is my religion? Where does my profit lie, and where my loss? Who is my friend, and who is my enemy? Is there one first principle or are there two? From whom is goodness, and from whom evil? From whom is light, and from whom darkness? From whom is fragrance, and from whom stench? From whom is order, and from whom disorder? From whom is mercy, and from whom pitilessness?'

(2)   Now it is faith that searches out causes, palpable and as they are, and then, acting as mediator by means of reason (passes them on).

So this must one know without venturing to doubt:
'I have come from the unseen world, nor was I always
of this world. I was created and have not always been.
I belong to Ohrmazd, not to Ahriman. I belong to
the gods, not to the demons, to the good, not to
the wicked. I am a man, not a demon, a creature of
Ohrmazd, not of Ahriman. My stock and lineage
is from Gayomart (the Zoroastrian Adam).' My
mother is Spandarmat, (the Earth), and my father
is Ohrmazd. My humanity is from Mashye and
Mashyaine who were the first seed and offspring
of Gayomart.

(3) To perform my function and to do my duty means
that I should believe that Ohrmazd is, was, and evermore shall be, that his Kingdom is undying, and that
he is infinite and pure; and that Ahriman is not, and is
destructible; that I myself belong to Ohrmazd and his
Bounteous Immortals, and that I have no connection
with Ahriman, the demons, and their associates.

(4) My first duty on earth is to confess the Religion, to
practise it, and to take part in its worship and to be
steadfast in it, to keep the Faith in the Good Religion of
the worshippers of Ohrmazd ever in my mind, and to
distinguish profit from loss, sin from good works, goodness from evil, light from darkness, and the worship of
Ohrmazd from the worship of the demons.

(5) My second duty is to take a wife and to procreate earthly
offspring, and to be strenuous and steadfast in this.

(6)   My third duty is to cultivate and till the soil;

(7)   my fourth to treat all livestock justly;

(8)   my fifth to spend a third of my days and nights in attending the seminary and consulting the wisdom of holy men, to spend a third of my days and nights in tilling the soil and in making it fruitful, and to spend the remaining third of my days and nights in eating, rest, and enjoyment.

(9)   I must have no doubt but that profit arises from good works, and loss from sin, that my friend is Ohrmazd and my enemy Ahriman, and that there is only one religious way.

(10) This one way is that of good thoughts, good words, and good deeds, the way of Heaven, of light and of purity, of the Infinite Creator, Ohrmazd, who was always and will ever be.

(11) There is also the other way of evil thoughts, evil words, and evil deeds, the way of darkness, and of the finiteness, utter misery, death, and wickedness which belong to the accursed Destructive Spirit (Ahriman) who once was not in this creation, and again will not be in the creation of Ohrmazd, and who in the end will be destroyed.

(12) I must have no doubt but that there are two first principles, one the Creator and the other the Destroyer.

(13) The Creator is Ohrmazd who is all goodness and all light:

(14) and the Destroyer is the accursed Destructive Spirit who is all wickedness and full of death, a liar and a deceiver.

(15) Equally I must have no doubt that all men are mortal except only Soshyans (the Saviour who will come at the end of time) and the seven beings who help him.

(16) I must have no doubt but that the soul will be severed from the body and that the body itself will be dissolved. Nor may I doubt the three nights judgement of the soul at death, the raising of the dead and the Final Body, the crossing of the Bridge of the Requiter, and the coming of Soshyans.

(17) I must observe the law of chivalry and the Religion of the Ancients, and I must preserve my thoughts in righteousness, my tongue in truth, and my hands in doing what is good.

(18) With all good men I must observe the law of chivalry,

(19) peace and concord in all good deeds I do.

(20) In my dealing with the good I must always behave according to justice and the dictates of the Good Religion.

(21) With whomsoever it may be, in past, present, and future time, I must act in a common virtue and in a common righteousness.

(22) Good deeds performed for the sake of the Law are of a higher value than those performed for one's own sake, and by them is salvation most assured.

(23) I declare that I have received the Good Religion of the worshippers of Ohrmazd and have no doubts

concerning it not for any bodily or spiritual comfort that it may bring, not for a pleasant life or for a long life, nor yet because I know that my consciousness must needs part company with my body. I shall never apostatise from the Good Religion of the worshippers of Ohrmazd, and I have no doubts concerning it.

(24) For it is plain that of thoughts, words, and deeds it is deeds only that are the criterion:

(25) for the will is unstable, thought is impalpable, but deeds are palpable indeed,

(26) and by the deeds that men do are they made known. In Man's body three roads have been laid out.

(27) On these three roads three angels have their dwelling, and three demons seek to waylay.

In thought Vahuman, (the Good Mind), has his dwelling, and Wrath seeks to waylay; in words Wisdom has its dwelling, and Heresy seeks to waylay; but in deeds the Bounteous Spirit, Ohrmazd, has his dwelling, and the Destructive Spirit, Ahriman, seeks to waylay.

(28) On these three roads Man must stand firm, nor may he give up his heavenly reward for the sake of worldly goods, wealth, or earthly desire.

(29) For the man who does not guard these three bastions within his body which I have mentioned, his thoughts proceed from evil thought, his words from evil speech, and his deeds from evil deeds.

(30) Next must I be thankful; and by thankfulness I mean gratitude for that it is within my power that my soul may not go to Hell.

(31) For when a man passes from the loins of his father into the womb of his mother, then does Astvihat, ('the Dissolver of Bones' and demon of death), secretly cast a halter round his neck which for his whole life's span cannot be shaken off, not through the power of a good spirit and not through the power of an evil spirit;

(32) but after he has passed away, that halter falls from off the neck of the man who is saved through the good deeds that he has done, but the man who is damned is dragged to Hell by that very halter.

(33) Whosoever is in the world must perform the office a certain number of times and must know what sins he is liable to commit with hand or foot, unless he be deaf or dumb in that case he cannot be accounted guilty. Should a deaf or dumb man perform a religious office, then it should be the *erpatastan* (the priest), and he should know the commentary on it.

(34) Fathers and mothers must teach their children this much concerning good works before they reach their fifteenth year. If they have taught them this much concerning good works, the parents may claim credit for any good deed the child does; but if the child has not been properly instructed, then the

parents are responsible for any sin it may commit on attaining majority.

(35) Be agreeable to good works and do not have any part in sin. Be grateful for good things, contented in adversity, long-suffering in affliction, zealous in the performance of your duty.

(36) Overcome doubts and unrighteous desires with reason.

(37) Overcome greed with contentment, anger with serenity, envy with benevolence, want with vigilance, strife with peace, falsehood with truth.

(38) Know that Heaven is the best place, that the kingdom of the spirit is the most pleasurable, that the mansions of the sky are the most luminous, that Paradise is a shining house, and the doing of good works brings great hope of the Final Body which does not pass away.

(39) So far as lies within your power, do not pay respect to evil men, for by commending what is wrong, evil enters into your body and good is driven out.

(40) Be diligent in the acquisition of learning, for learning is the seed of knowledge, and its fruit is wisdom, and wisdom rules both worlds.

(41) Concerning this it has been said that learning is an adornment in prosperity, a protection in hard times, a ready helper in affliction, a guide in distress.

(42) Do not mock anyone at all; for the man who mocks will himself be mocked, will lose his dignity (*khwarr*)

and be execrated; and rarely indeed will he have a
decent or warlike son.

(43) Seek every day the company of good men to ask
their advice, for he who makes a habit of seeking the
company of good men, will be blessed with a greater
share of virtue and holiness.

(44) Go three times a day to the Fire Temple and do
homage to the Fire; for he who makes a habit of
going to the Fire Temple and of doing homage
to the Fire, will be blessed with a greater share of
both worldly wealth and of holiness.

(45) Take great care never to vex your father and mother
or your superior lest your body become ill-famed
thereby and your soul see damnation.

(46) Know that of all the countless adversities that the
accursed Destructive Spirit devised these three are
the most grievous, the obstruction of the sight of the
eye, deafness of the ear, and thirdly the Lie of discord.

(47) For it is revealed that for this reason does the Sun
issue his command to men on earth three times a day.

(48) At dawn he says, 'Ohrmazd ever bids you who are
men to be diligent in the doing of good works so that
I may bestow earthly life upon you.'

(49) At midday he says, 'Be diligent in seeking out a
wife, in the procreation of children, and in your
other duties, for until the Final Body comes to pass
the Destructive Spirit and his abortions will not be
separated from this world.'

(50) At eventide he says, 'Repent of the sins you have committed that I may have compassion on you.' For it is revealed that just as the light of the Sun comes down to earth, so do his words come to earth.

(51) In this material world do not think, say or do what is wrong (false) in thought, word, or deed.

(52) Through the power of the gods, and by way of wisdom and by consultation with the Religion be vigilant and zealous for good works, and consider that since the value of good works is so great and limitless, the Destructive Spirit strives his utmost to conceal this truth and to cause you misery, and Ohrmazd strives his utmost to reveal the truth. Whosoever has knowledge of the Religion, let him be diligent in the doing of good works and be forever steadfast therein.

(53) At the end of this millennium when the wickedness of the demons knows no limit and the Religion of Ohrmazd is much reduced and that of the unrighteous is predominant, when discussions concerning the Law and Religion between good and righteous men who know their duty have ceased, when the deeds of Ahriman and the demons are done openly, and the sign of this will be that there will be a general retrogression when creatures will be destroyed, those who break contracts and who have taken the part of the demons and opposed the religion will go free, and when throughout the length and breadth of the

lands which acknowledge the Law of Ohrmazd all good creatures will despair on account of wicked tyrants (*azhidahākān*), then every man must add to his (inner) peace through the power of Vahuman, the Good Mind, consult with Wisdom through the Religion, search out the way of holiness by wisdom, rejoice his soul by means of generosity, show honour to rank by benevolence, seek a good name by manliness, collect friends by humility, make hope acceptable by long-suffering, store up (for himself) goodness by temperance (*khem*), and prepare the way to bright heaven by righteousness; for there shall he enjoy the fruits of his good works.

(54) The body is mortal but the soul is immortal. Do good works, for the soul is real, not the body, the next world is real, not this world.

(55) Do not abandon the care of the soul and forget it for the body's sake.

(56) Out of respect for persons and out of forgetfulness that all the goods of this world must perish, do not lust after anything that will bring punishment on your body and retribution on your soul. Desire rather those things whose fruit is an everlasting joy.

(57) Doing good is born of the zeal of prayer, prayer of desire, desire of intellect, intellect of knowledge of the other world; and knowledge of the other world is a weapon that was and is and evermore shall be. By it He is known Who creates all things anew, Who teaches

all things, Who ordains all that should be done, Who wills the good of all in this world and the next.

The Doctrine of the Middle Path or 'Mean' is set out in a Pahlavi text as follows:

Shrikand Gumani Vazar, Chapter I, Verses 11–19

(11) The Religion of omniscience is like a mighty tree (12) with one trunk, two great boughs, three branches, four off-branches, and five roots. (13) And the one trunk is the Mean, (14) the two great boughs are action and abstention, (15) the three branches are humat, hūkht, and huvarsht, that is, good thoughts, good words, and good deeds. (16) The four off-branches are the four religious castes by which the Religion and secular life are (both) maintained, (17) the priesthood, the warrior caste, the caste of husbandmen, and the caste of artisans. (18) The five roots are the five (degrees of) government whose names in Religion are *manpat* (householder), *vispat* (village headman), *zandpat* (tribal chieftain), *dehpat* (provincial governor) and the *Zarathrushtōtom* (the highest religious authority and representative of Zoroaster on earth). (19) (Over and above these) is another, the Chief of all chiefs, that is the King of Kings, the governor of the (whole) world.

The Story of Two Primeval Spirits and Creation

The story of the two primeval spirits and the creation of the world is recounted in greatest detail in the first chapter of a ninth-century book known as the *Bundahishn* (Book of the Primal Creation).

In this book, God is originally finite, limited as He is by the opposite principle, Ahriman. So he would have remained for all eternity had not Ahriman been what he is, an aggressor, and an ill-informed aggressor at that. The mere fact that Ahriman attacks makes it possible for God to become infinite, for this enables Ohrmazd to counter-attack in self-defence. It is the attack of Ahriman that evokes the defence of Ohrmazd, and it is the disorder in Ahriman himself that finally brings about his own destruction. This story of the cosmic struggle results not only in the destruction of Ahriman, but in the perfecting of God: the good Spirit who was finite, emerges as infinite. Man, then, in fighting on the side of Ohrmazd, is fighting for his own immortality, his share in the Final Body, which is infinite.

In the beginning, the two antagonists are poised for battle, the one 'omniscient and good', and the other the aggressor, 'whose will is to smite'. Ohrmazd foresees the attack and creates an 'ideal' or spiritual creation 'without thought, without movement, without touch' with which to defend himself; 'such creation as was needful for his instrument'. One may well ask who or what this 'instrument' is. It appears to be Vayu or the Void, for Vayu who appears both as a deity and as the Void is elsewhere described as 'the instrument he (Ohrmazd) needed for the deed'. The Void, then, is enlisted by Ohrmazd in advance on his side. Creation and the Void are complementary, and once the battle begins, Vayu, the Void, is galvanized into life; it is the force which breaks down opposition.

Meanwhile, Ahriman is not idle. He has seen the light and would destroy it, so he sets about forging his own weapons in the shape of demons. Ohrmazd offers peace which is summarily rejected. As a compromise, then, the two spirits agree to do battle for 9000 years at the end of which, as Ohrmazd knows, Ahriman will be utterly destroyed.

So passed the first three thousand years of the great 'Cosmic Year' which lasts for 12,000 years. The battle proper begins with Ohrmazd chanting the 'Yatha Ahu Vairyo', the key prayer of the Zoroastrians. The mere recital of this prayer reveals to Ahriman that all is already over, and that his ultimate annihilation is certain. He swoons and falls back into the darkness where he lies unconscious for three thousand years.

During Ahriman's indisposition, Ohrmazd quietly proceeds to create the two worlds—the world of spirit and the world of matter—in the next 3000 years. The two creations are complementary. On the spiritual side stand Ohrmazd and the six Amesha Spentas, the Bounteous Immortals, his archangels who are at the same time aspects of himself; on the other side stand Man and the six other material creations which are there to help him. Man himself is Ohrmazd's deputy on Earth. Each of the six Amesha Spentas also takes one of the material creations under his special patronage. The names of the Amesha Spentas are Vohuman (Good Mind), Artvahisht (Righteousness or Truth), Shahrevar (the power of the kingdom of God), Spandarmat (Right-Mindedness who is in fact identical with the earth), Hurvat (Wholeness or Salvation), and Ameredat (Immortality).

The six material creations are, in the order that they were created: the sky, water, the Earth, plants, the Primal Bull, and Gayomart, the First Man; and lastly, fire, which 'permeated all six elements'. In the third chapter of the *Bundahishn*, God and each of the Amesha Spentas adopts one material creation; Ohrmazd adopts Man; Vohuman, cattle; Artvahisht, fire; Spandarmat, the Earth; Hurvat, water; and Ameredat, plants. Shahrevar adopts metals. Each material creation, then, stands under a tutelary deity. The two worlds are connected, and in close cooperation they both stand ready to face Ahriman again.

Ahriman, then, revived by the primeval Whore's promise to destroy the dignity of the Blessed Man, delivers his attack on the material creation of Ohrmazd. He bursts through the periphery of the sky and rends it, defiles the waters and makes them brackish, attacks the Earth by letting loose upon it all manner of filthy and creeping things, poisons the plants and brings disease upon the 'lone-created Bull' so that he sickens and dies. Next, he attacks Gayomart, the Blessed Man himself, with the Demon of Death and a thousand of his accomplices and afflicts mankind with greed and want, pain, disease, lust and sloth. Yet, Gayomart lives for thirty years after the attack was launched. During these thirty years, it must be assumed, his unholy union with the primeval Whore was consummated.

Lastly, Ahriman attacks the holy fire and befouls it with smoke. At this point, Ahriman achieves his highest power. One thing, however, he had forgotten. Though he had rent the sky and come upon the Earth from its lower side, the sky was able to close the hole and Ahriman found himself entrapped in the material Universe till the end of time. 'And the Spirit of the Sky said to the Destructive Spirit, "Till the end of Time must I watch over thee so as not to suffer thee to escape".' Trapped then as he is in the snare of the sky, he is set upon by the powers of light until he and his demon host are routed and hurled into Hell, which is in the middle of the Earth. Creation, however, has been definitely corrupted, and Ahriman remains within it to continue his abominable works until the Resurrection and the Final Body when all is made good 'and neither the Destructive Spirit nor his creation will exist'.

The Wisdom of Adarbad Maraspand

A great Chief Priest, Adarbad Maraspand, lived in the fourth century CE at the time of the Sasanian Emperor Shapur II. He left behind a number of wisdom sayings based on Zoroastrian scriptures, some of which are set out below.

Do not be overjoyed in good times nor overdistressed in bad times, for the good fortune of Time turns to misfortune and the misfortune of Time turns to good fortune, and there is no 'up' that has not been preceded by a 'down,' and no 'down' that is not followed by an 'up,'

Do not be gluttonous (varanik) in eating your food,

Do not partake of all foods. Do not be over-hasty to attend the feasts and banquets of the great lest you return from them ashamed.

For there are four things which are most harmful to the body of mortal men and make them have wrong ideas about their body. One is to glory in one's strength. One is the luxury of pride which leads one to pick a quarrel with a well-established (hangat) man. One is the case of the elderly man with a puerile character who weds an adolescent girl; and one is the case of the young man who weds an old woman.

It should be known that love of one's fellow men proceeds from a balanced mind (bavandak-menishnih), and good character from being nicely spoken.

And I say unto you, my son, that of all the things that give help to man wisdom is the best.

(1)   These are some of the sayings of Adhurbadh, son of Mahraspand, spoken by him on his death-bed to the people. He taught them (on these lines): Remember (what I say now) most particularly (pat dakhshak) and act accordingly. Do not hoard against the day when you may be in need.

(2)   Strive to hoard up only righteousness (*ahrayih*), (that is) virtuous deeds, for of (all) the things that one may hoard, only righteousness is good.

(3)   Do not harbour vengeance in your thoughts lest your enemies catch up with you.

(4)   Consider rather what injury, harm, and destruction you are liable to suffer by smiting your enemy in vengeance and how you will brood over vengeance in your heart (*varom*). Do not smite your enemy in vengeance, for it is plain enough that whoever puts vengeance even for a trifling thing out of his mind, will be spared the greatest terrors at the Bridge of the Judge.

(5)   Whether you are defendant or plaintiff (at a court of law) tell the truth so that you may be the more certain of acquittal at the trial.

(6)   For it is clear that by giving true witness a man will be saved, and damned will be the man who perjures himself.

(7)   Show moderation in your eating (and drinking) so that you may live long;

(8)   for moderation in eating (and drinking) is good for the body as moderation in speech is good for the soul.

(9)   Though a man be very poor in the goods of this world, he is (nevertheless) rich if there is moderation in his character.

(10) Pay more attention to your soul than to your belly, for the man who fills his belly usually brings disorder on his spirit.

(11) Take a wife from among your kin so that your lineage may be more protracted;

(12) for most of the disorder and vengeful spirit and loss from which the creatures of Ohrmazd have suffered has been caused by the giving of one's daughters (to the sons of strangers) and the asking of the daughters of strangers in marriage for one's sons. So does a family die out.

(13) Abstain rigorously from eating the flesh of kine and all domestic animals (*gospandan*) lest you be made to face a strict reckoning in this world and the next;

(14) for by eating the flesh of kine and other domestic animals, you involve your hand in sin, and thereby think, speak, and do what is sinful;

(15) for though you eat but a mouthful, you involve your hand in sin, and though a camel be slain by another man in another place it is as if you, who eat its flesh had slain it with your own hand.

(16) Make the traveller welcome so that you yourself may receive a heartier welcome in this world and the next;

(17) for he who gives, receives, and receives more abundantly. Seat yourself at a banquet where your host bids you be seated, for the best place is where a good man sits.

(18) Do not strive for high office, for the man who strives for high office usually brings disorder on his spirit.

(19) Live in harmony with virtue and do not consent to sin. Be thankful for good fortune and contented in adversity, avoid an enemy; do not cause harm in doing good works; do not aid and abet evil.

(20) Even should the most fearful calamity befall you, do not doubt concerning the gods and the Religion.

(21) Do not be unduly glad when good fortune attends you,

(22) and do not be unduly downcast when misfortune befalls you.

(23) Be contented in adversity, patient in disaster. Do not put your trust in life, but put your trust in good works;

(24) for the good man's good works are his advocate and an evil man's works are his accuser,

(25) and of thoughts, words, and deeds, deeds are the most perfect.

(26) For there is no misfortune which has befallen me, Adhurbadh, son of Mahraspand, from which I have not derived six kinds of comfort.

(27) First, when a misfortune befell me, I was thankful that it was no worse.

(28) Secondly, when a misfortune fell not upon my soul but upon my body, (I was thankful), for it seemed better that it should befall the body rather than the soul.

(29) Thirdly, I was thankful that of all the misfortunes that are due to me one at least had passed.

(30) Fourthly I was thankful that I was so good a man that the accursed and damnable Ahriman and the demons should bring misfortune on my body on account of my goodness.

(31) Fifthly I was thankful that since whoever commits an evil deed, will be made to suffer for it either in his own person or in his children, it was I myself who paid the price, not my children.

(32) Sixthly, I was thankful that since all the harm that the accused Ahriman and his demons can do to the creatures of Ohrmazd is limited, any misfortune that befalls me is a loss to Ahriman's treasury, and he cannot inflict it a second time on some other good man.

(33) Abstain rigorously from churlishnes, self-will, enmity to the good, anger, rapine, calumny, and lying so that your body be not ill-famed and your soul damned.

(34) Do not plot evil against the evil man, for the evil man reaps the fruit of his own bad actions.

(35) In order to bear with evil men, keep the power of goodness in mind and make it your model.

(36) Has there ever been a man who associated with evil men who did not regret it in the end?

(37) Do good simply because it is good. Goodness is a real good (*nevak*) since even evil men extol it.

(38) Do whatever you know to be good and do not do anything that you know to be not good.

(39) Do not do to others anything that does not seem good to yourself.

(40) Do not underestimate the value of confessing your sins of omission to the religious judges, of submitting to the disciplinary whip.

(41) You have only one name, you are men. Do not pay attention to both the desires of the body and the soul;

(42) for the body and the soul do not both have the same desire.

(43) The bodily desires of the body should be satisfied and the soul-desires of the soul.

(44) Never commit a sin out of vengeance, but always strive your utmost to do good works.

(45) Do not forsake the righteous law out of lust.

(46) Do not violently strike innocent people because you are angry with someone.

(47) Do not be false to a contract out of vengeance lest you be caught in the consequences of your own actions.

(48) Put not your trust in fools lest you have cause to be ashamed and to repent.

(49) Do not tell your secrets to fools lest all your toiling be fruitless.

(50) Do not take orders from the crafty lest you meet with ruin.

(51) For these four things are most useful to men, wisdom (combined with) courage, vision (combined with) knowledge, wealth (combined with) generosity, and good words (combined with) good deeds.

(52) For courage divorced from wisdom is very death in a man's body;

(53) vision divorced from knowledge is like a pictured image of a body;

(54) wealth divorced from generosity is like a treasure of Ahriman;

(55) good words divorced from good deeds are manifest unbelief (*ahramoghik*).

(56) The signs of the unbeliever are six; he has the outward appearance of good character, but does the works that beseem a bad character; he performs the liturgy correctly, but does evil; he 'talks big' to others, but is himself stingy though seeming generous; he is a giver of evil gifts and patient of abuse; his thoughts, words, and deeds do not agree.

(57) Do not say anything that is not specifically of profit except as a joke (*huramīk*), and when joking consider the time and the occasion.

(58) For wisdom guards the tongue, the body's fruit is civilised behaviour, and the reward of virtue is Heaven and the receiving and giving of the fruits of the earth;

(59) for all forms of courage need wisdom, wisdom knowledge, knowledge experience. To be respected

one must have a good name. All actions depend on the proper time and place, while wealth needs to be received and given away, and all enjoyment depends on freedom from fear.

(60) Do not rejoice overmuch when good fortune attends you, and do not grieve overmuch when misfortune overtakes you,

(61) for both good fortune and misfortune must befall man.

(62) Be grateful to the gods for any good fortune that may befall you in this world and share it with the gods and with good men. Leave all such things to the gods, for any reward that is due to you will come of its own accord from the place whence it must proceed,

(63) Till the earth and do good, for all men live and are nourished by the tilling of Spandarmat, the Earth.

(64) Do not sin against water, fire, kine, or other domestic animals, or against the dog and the dog species, lest you find the way to Heaven and Paradise closed to you.

(65) Do good and keep your doors open to any who may come from far or near, for he who does not do good and does not keep his doors open, will find the door of Heaven and of Paradise closed.

(66) Be zealous in the pursuit of culture, for culture is an adornment in prosperity, a protection in distress, a ready helper in calamity, and becomes a habit in adversity.

(67) When you have learnt something, put it into practice, for the man who knows a lot and believes little is the greater sinner.

(68) The wisdom of a learned man, if unaccompanied by goodness, turns to injustice and his intelligence turns to unbelief.

(69) Do not mock anyone at all, for he who mocks himself becomes the object of mockery, he loses his dignity (*khwarr*) and is execrated, and only rarely will he have a decent and warlike son.

(70) Go every day to wherever good men gather together to consult them,

(71) for whoever goes most frequently to where good men gather together for the purpose of consultation, receives a greater share of virtue and holiness.

(72) Go to the Fire-Temple three times a day and recite the liturgy to the fire,

(73) for whoever goes most frequently to the Fire-Temple and recites the liturgy to the fire, receives a greater portion of worldly goods and of holiness.

(74) Keep your body rigorously aloof from the sin of the Lie, from a woman in her menses, and from a harlot in milk so that your soul may not be involved in the hurt such evil does to the body.

(75) Do not leave any sin for which penance is demanded (unconfessed) even for a moment so that the pure Religion of the worshippers of Ohrmazd may not be your enemy.

(76) The body is mortal, but the soul does not pass away. Do good, for the soul really is, not the body; spirit really is, not matter.

(77) Out of respect for the body do not neglect your soul; and do not, out of respect for anyone, forget that the things of this world are transitory. Desire nothing that will bring penance on your body and punishment on your soul.

(78) Do not, out of affection for anyone, neglect the respect due to your soul so that you may not have to suffer a grievous punishment against your will.

Judaism

Judaism is one the oldest monotheistic religions of the world and begins with Abraham. Abraham himself is a descendant of Adam, the first man, and Eve, the first woman, and their son, Seth. These descendants are listed in the Old Testament, which is a compilation belonging to a larger compilation, the Bible. The Old Testament comprises thirty-nine books. The first important event, chronologically, is the great flood which takes place during the time of Noah, who builds an ark and takes a pair of every species of animal and bird, so that finally, when the great flood subsides, living beings do not get wiped out.

Abraham was commanded by God to go to the land of Canaan and promised him that from his son, Isaac, he would make a great nation. Abraham first went to Egypt to escape a famine and then stayed in a place called Hebron. God tested Abraham several times. One test was the sacrifice of his son Isaac, born to Abraham's wife, Sara, long after she couldn't bear children. Abraham was willing to do so but God stayed his hand and provided a lamb who was sacrificed instead. Abraham had previously fathered another son named Ishmael, who was older than Isaac, through a slave girl called Hagar. It is from Ishmael that the Arab tribes descended and Islam as a religion came to the world. Isaac in turn begot two sons: Esau and Jacob.

The history of the Jews revolves around Jacob, as Jacob succeeded Isaac instead of his elder son Esau. Jacob, also called Israel, since he wrestled with an angel at night, produced twelve sons who were the progenitors of the twelve tribes of Israel. These twelve tribes then occupied what was later known as the northern kingdom, Israel, and Judah, the southern kingdom. The single most important or central figure in Judaism is Prophet Moses. He was the son of a Jewish mother in Egypt and, as a baby, was put into a little basket and sent down a stream. He was found by the Pharaoh's daughter who adopted him and named him Moses. When he grew up, he was tending the flock of his father-in-law when an angel appeared before him in a burning bush and the Lord spoke to him from the bush saying that he, Moses, had to deliver the people of Israel from their bondage in Egypt to a Promised Land. God sent nine plagues to Egypt to soften the Pharaoh's hard heart and when these failed to move him, finally sent the tenth plague where all the firstborns of the Egyptians were killed. At this, the Jews were allowed to leave Egypt. Moses then took them through the Red Sea, which was made to part, and soon after, swallowed up the Pharaoh and his army who were in hot pursuit of the Jews. In commemoration of this, the Jews hold a Passover feast every year as an angel 'passed over' every Jewish house so as to save every firstborn Jewish child from death. The Book of Esther produced another important festival, that of Purim, where the Jews were able to triumph over their enemies in Persia at the time of Emperor Xerxes.

After wandering across the desert, the Jews occupied an area in Canaan. God then spoke to Moses in the desert at Mount Sinai and told him that the Jews must keep their covenant with Abraham since they were the chosen people, chosen to be a beacon of light to the world in ethical behaviour and conduct. The Ten Commandments were then given to Moses in tablet form for the Jews to follow. These commandments are simple and direct, and, if followed, lead to ethical conduct of the highest order. The Commandments are:

1. Thou shalt have no other gods before me.
2. Thou shalt not make unto thee any graven image, or any likeness of any thing that is in heaven above, or that is in the earth beneath, or that is in the water under the earth.
3. Thou shalt not take the name of the Lord thy God in vain; for the Lord will not hold him guiltless that taketh his name in vain.
4. Remember the Sabbath day, to keep it holy. (The Sabbath Day was the day on which God himself rested after creating the Earth.)
5. Honour thy father and thy mother: that thy days may be long upon the land which the Lord thy God giveth thee.

6. Thou shalt not kill.

7. Thou shalt not commit adultery.

8. Thou shalt not steal.

9. Thou shalt not bear false witness against thy neighbour.

10. Thou shalt not covet thy neighbour's house, thou shalt not covet thy neighbour's wife, nor his manservant, nor his maidservant, nor his ox, nor his ass, nor any thing that is thy neighbour's.

Moses himself was only given a sighting of the Promised Land before he died and it was Joshua who actually took the Jews into the Promised Land which they then occupied. Joshua, after having led the Jews to the Promised Land in Canaan, died. After him, the Jews were led by a series of 'judges', the most famous of whom is Samson, who 'judged' them for a period of twenty years. In his youth, Samson had married a Philistine woman and quarrelled with her tribe because of this marriage, having killed a thousand of them with the jawbone of an ass. However, he was enticed by another Philistine woman, Delilah, who learnt the secret of his strength which lay in his long hair. While he slept, she cut his hair after which he was captured, blinded and imprisoned by the Philistines. It was only when his hair grew again that he went to their temple, held the two supporting pillars and broke them with brute strength, thereby killing himself and a large number of people in the temple.

After the judges, the last being a priest called Samuel, the period of the kings started with the reign of Saul, who ruled for twenty years. It is during his reign that there was another attack by the Philistines, their leader being a giant called Goliath. At this point, a young lad David was called upon to fight Goliath and he slew Goliath by hitting him with a stone from a sling. The Bible tells us of the conflict between David and Saul and how David finally became king. David, in turn, fathered many sons but it was a younger son, Solomon, from a Hittite woman called Bathsheba, who then ruled. Solomon's importance to the Jews is in the fact that he built their first temple at Jerusalem.

After Solomon's reign, the country was divided into the northern kingdom, where ten tribes lived (called Israel), and the southern kingdom, where two tribes lived (called Judah). Israel was destroyed in 722 BCE by the Assyrians. As a result of this, the ten tribes scattered all over the world and were lost to history. It was only the tribes of Judah and Benjamin who continued to live in Judah and stayed on till the sixth century BCE when they in turn were destroyed by the Babylonian king, Nebuchadnezzar. Solomon's Temple itself was destroyed and a large number of Jews were deported to Babylon. Their saviour came in the form of Cyrus the Great, the King of Persia, who in turn conquered Babylon and decreed that funds be given to rebuild their temple. This temple was rebuilt in the reign of Darius the Great, as is recounted in the Book of Ezra, and the period of the second temple then saw the Jews divided into Pharisees and Sadducees. The Pharisees were Jews who were influenced by Persian eschatology so as to start believing in an afterlife which was different from what they were taught. The Sadducees, continuing the old tradition, taught that once a Jew died, he or she went to a place called Sheol, a place of ultimate repose. The Pharisees replaced Sheol with a heaven and a hell, dependent on one's deeds, and a judgement day and a resurrection on Earth.

The history of the Jews then goes on from the Persian era to the Seleucid era after Alexander's conquest of Persia; and finally, to the Roman era. The second temple built in the sixth century BCE was embellished by King Herod the Great, some time around the birth of Christ, and it is this temple which was finally destroyed in 70 CE by a Roman general named Titus (who later became the emperor). After this, the Jews scattered all over the world until they finally came together forming the state of Israel in 1948.

Jewish beliefs centre strongly around one God who has made a covenant with his people. This covenant was repeatedly breached as the Jews worshipped the gods of neighbouring people as well. A very large number of prophets have been sent down through Jewish history from the time of Moses right up to the time of the destruction of the second temple in 70 CE. Prominent among these prophets is Elijah, who stopped idol worship in the form of a Canaanite God called Ba'al, by proving that the God of Israel was superior to this God Ba'al, and by utterly destroying the priests of Ba'al. Elisha succeeded Elijah and continued his work. There were other prominent prophets such as Isaiah, Jeremiah, Ezekiel and Daniel, and some minor prophets who continued with the covenant which was repeatedly breached by the Jews resulting in the destruction of their temple and their being driven away from Judah.

The Jews place their faith in the Torah, which is the first five books of the Old Testament, all of which are said to have been composed by Moses, and the later Talmud, which consists of the Mishnah, which is a compendium of the oral sayings of Moses and the Gemara, which is writings and explanations of the Mishnah. One of its most famous sons, Moses Maimonides, lived in Spain in the twelfth century CE. He wrote a treatise on the Jewish canon and came out with thirteen principles of faith, which he believed encompassed the essence of Jewish teaching. They are as follows:

1. Belief in the existence of the Creator, who is perfect in every manner of existence and is the Primary Cause of all that exists.
2. The belief in God's absolute and unparalleled unity.
3. The belief in God's non-corporeality, nor that He will be affected by any physical occurrences, such as movement, or rest, or dwelling.
4. The belief in God's eternity.
5. The imperative to worship God exclusively and no foreign false gods.
6. The belief that God communicates with man through prophecy.

7. The belief in the primacy of the prophecy of Moses our teacher.

8. The belief in the divine origin of the Torah.

9. The belief in the immutability of the Torah.

10. The belief in God's omniscience and providence.

11. The belief in divine reward and retribution.

12. The belief in the arrival of the Messiah and the messianic era.

13. The belief in the resurrection of the dead.

The Jews are governed by strict dietary laws contained in the Book of Leviticus, part of the Torah.

Since there is no central authority in Judaism, it was free to develop in unorthodox ways. Judaism as originally preached did not believe in an afterlife beyond going to the shadowy sheol. Later writings, especially the Kabbalah, incorporated a doctrine of reincarnation which is not consistent with mainstream Judaism, as practised today.

Christianity

The person of Jesus Christ forms the fulcrum of Christianity. His story is told in four Gospel accounts that are to be found in the Bible, the second portion of which is called the New Testament. Three of these accounts are said to be synoptic for the reason that they broadly agree with one another. The Gospel according to St Matthew is by a tax collector who became one of the twelve apostles of Jesus. The second, the Gospel of St Mark, is by a disciple of St Peter who was the foremost disciple or apostle of Jesus. The third, the Gospel of St Luke, constitutes Jesus's life and sayings through the eyes of Luke, who was a physician and a follower of St Paul. And the last, the Gospel of St John, is written after the three synoptic gospels and gives a different version of Jesus's life and teachings. John was the youngest of the twelve apostles to follow Jesus.

Jesus's birth is said to be miraculous, from a virgin. An angel of the Lord, Gabriel, comforted Jesus's mother, Mary, and told Mary's husband, Joseph, that the child would be an immaculate conception, born to save people from their sins. Three magi or Zoroastrian priests came from the East to bless baby Jesus, bringing with them gifts of frankincense, myrrh and gold. Herod the Great, at that point the ruler of Judea under the Roman Empire, was told that he would be killed by this child. Herod consequently ordered the death of all infants in that region. As a result of this, Joseph and Mary fled with baby Jesus to Egypt until Herod's death after which they returned to Judea, where Jesus grew up, until the age of twelve. After this, the Bible says nothing about him till he turned thirty. This is when his cousin John the Baptist first proclaimed that he had come in order to make way for Jesus. John the Baptist then preached to his people, introducing Jesus to the populace of Judea by baptizing him in the river Jordan. Before he began his ministry, Jesus spent forty days fasting in the wilderness at which time the devil appeared with various temptations. To each temptation, Jesus replied, 'Thou shalt worship the Lord thy God, and him only shalt thou serve' (KJV, Luke 4:8).

Jesus then began his ministry and went all around Judea preaching 'Repent: for the kingdom of heaven is at hand' (KJV, Matt. 4:17). He then made two brothers—Simon, who was called Peter, and Andrew, both fishermen, his first disciples. He went around preaching and healing persons with all kinds of ailments. Slowly and steadily, great multitudes of people followed him. At this point, Jesus preached on a mountain and proclaimed what is known to the world as the Sermon on the Mount. The sermon is a perfect summary of his teachings, and is reproduced below:

Blessed are the poor in spirit: for theirs is the kingdom of heaven. Blessed are they that mourn: for they shall be comforted.

Blessed are the meek: for they shall inherit the earth.

Blessed are they which do hunger and thirst after righteousness: for they shall be filled.

Blessed are the merciful: for they shall obtain mercy. Blessed are the pure in heart: for they shall see God.

Blessed are the peacemakers: for they shall be called the children of God.

Blessed are they which are persecuted for righteousness' sake: for theirs is the kingdom of heaven.

Blessed are ye, when men shall revile you, and persecute you, and shall say all manner of evil against you falsely, for my sake.

Rejoice, and be exceeding glad: for great is your reward in heaven: for so persecuted they the prophets which were before you.

But woe unto you that are rich! for ye have received your consolation.

Woe unto you that are full! for ye shall hunger. Woe unto you that laugh now! for ye shall mourn and weep.

Woe unto you, when all men shall speak well of you! for so did their fathers to the false prophets. Ye are the salt of the earth: but if the salt have lost his savour, wherewith shall it be salted? it is thenceforth good for nothing, but to be cast out, and to be trodden under foot of men.

Ye are the light of the world. A city that is set on an hill cannot be hid.

Neither do men light a candle, and put it under a bushel, but on a candlestick; and it giveth light unto all that are in the house.

Let your light so shine before men, that they may see your good works, and glorify your Father which is in heaven. Think not that I am come to destroy the law, or the prophets: I am not come to destroy, but to fulfil.

For verily I say unto you, Till heaven and earth pass, one jot or one tittle shall in no wise pass from the law, till all be fulfilled.

Whosoever therefore shall break one of these least commandments, and shall teach men so, he shall be called the least in the kingdom of heaven: but whosoever shall do and teach them, the same shall be called great in the kingdom of heaven.

For I say unto you, That except your righteousness shall exceed the righteousness of the scribes and Pharisees, ye shall in no case enter into the kingdom of heaven. Ye have heard that it was said by them of old time, Thou shalt not kill; and whosoever shall kill shall be in danger of the judgement:

But I say unto you, That whosoever is angry with his brother without a cause shall be in danger of the judgement: and whosoever shall say to his brother, Raca, shall be in danger of the council: but whosoever shall say, Thou fool, shall be in danger of hell fire.

Therefore if thou bring thy gift to the altar, and there rememberest that thy brother hath ought against thee;

Leave there thy gift before the altar, and go thy way; first be reconciled to thy brother, and then come and offer thy gift.

Agree with thine adversary quickly, whiles thou art in the way with him; lest at any time the adversary deliver thee to the judge, and the judge deliver thee to the officer, and thou be cast into prison.

Verily I say unto thee, Thou shalt by no means come out thence, till thou hast paid the uttermost farthing. Ye have heard that it was said by them of old time, Thou shalt not commit adultery:

But I say unto you, That whosoever looketh on a woman to lust after her hath committed adultery with her already in his heart.

And if thy right eye offend thee, pluck it out, and cast it from thee: for it is profitable for thee that one of thy members should perish, and not that thy whole body should be cast into hell.

And if thy right hand offend thee, cut it off, and cast it from thee: for it is profitable for thee that one of thy members should perish, and not that thy whole body should be cast into hell.

It hath been said, Whosoever shall put away his wife, let him give her a writing of divorcement:

But I say unto you, That whosoever shall put away his wife, saving for the cause of fornication, causeth her to commit adultery: and whosoever shall marry her that is divorced committeth adultery. Again, ye have heard that it hath been said by them of old time, Thou shalt not forswear thyself, but shalt perform unto the Lord thine oaths:

But I say unto you, Swear not at all; neither by heaven; for it is God's throne:

Nor by the earth; for it is his footstool: neither by Jerusalem; for it is the city of the great King.

Neither shalt thou swear by thy head, because thou canst not make one hair white or black.

But let your communication be, Yea, yea; Nay, nay: for whatsoever is more than these cometh of evil. Ye have heard that it hath been said, An eye for an eye, and a tooth for a tooth:

But I say unto you, That ye resist not evil: but whosoever shall smite thee on thy right cheek, turn to him the other also.

And if any man will sue thee at the law, and take away thy coat, let him have thy cloak also.

And whosoever shall compel thee to go a mile, go with him twain.

Give to him that asketh thee, and from him that would borrow of thee turn not thou away. Ye have heard that it hath been said, Thou shalt love thy neighbour, and hate thine enemy.

But I say unto you, Love your enemies, bless them that curse you, do good to them that hate you, and pray for them that despitefully use you, and persecute you;

That ye may be the children of your Father which is in heaven: for he maketh his sun to rise on the evil and on the good, and sendeth rain on the just and on the unjust.

For if ye love them which love you, what reward have ye? do not even the publicans the same?

And if ye salute your brethren only, what do ye more than others? do not even the publicans so?

And if ye lend to them of whom ye hope to receive, what thank have ye? for sinners also lend to sinners, to receive as much again.

But love ye your enemies, and do good, and lend, hoping for nothing again; and your reward shall be great, and ye shall be the children of the Highest: for he is kind unto the unthankful and to the evil.

Be ye therefore merciful, as your Father also is merciful.

Take heed that ye do not your alms before men, to be seen of them: otherwise ye have no reward of your Father which is in heaven.

Therefore when thou doest thine alms, do not sound a trumpet before thee, as the hypocrites do in the synagogues and in the streets, that they may have glory of men. Verily I say unto you, They have their reward.

But when thou doest alms, let not thy left hand know what thy right hand doeth:

That thine alms may be in secret: and thy Father which seeth in secret hinself shall reward thee openly. And when thou prayest, thou shalt not be as the hypocrites are: for they love to pray standing in the synagogues and in the corners of the streets, that they may be seen of men. Verily I say unto you, They have their reward.

But thou, when thou prayest, enter into thy closet, and when thou hast shut thy door, pray to thy Father which is in secret; and thy Father which seeth in secret shall reward thee openly.

But when ye pray, use not vain repetitions, as the heathen do: for they think that they shall be heard for their much speaking.

Be not ye therefore like unto them: for your Father knoweth what things ye have need of, before ye ask him.

After this manner therefore pray ye: Our Father which art in heaven, Hallowed be thy name.

Thy kingdom come, Thy will be done in earth, as it is in heaven. Give us this day our daily bread.

And forgive us our debts, as we forgive our debtors.

And lead us not into temptation, but deliver us from evil: For thine is the kingdom, and the power, and the glory, for ever. Amen.

For if ye forgive men their trespasses, your heavenly Father will also forgive you:

But if ye forgive not men their trespasses, neither will your Father forgive your trespasses. Moreover when ye fast, be not, as the hypocrites, of a sad countenance: for they disfigure their faces, that they may appear unto men to fast. Verily I say unto you, They have their reward.

But thou, when thou fastest, anoint thine head, and wash thy face;

That thou appear not unto men to fast, but unto thy Father which is in secret: and thy Father, which seeth in secret, shall reward thee openly. Lay not up for yourselves treasures upon earth, where moth and rust doth corrupt, and where thieves break through and steal:

But lay up for yourselves treasures in heaven, where neither moth nor rust doth corrupt, and where thieves do not break through nor steal:

For where your treasure is, there will your heart be also.

The light of the body is the eye: if therefore thine eye be single, thy whole body shall be full of light.

But if thine eye be evil, thy whole body shall be full of darkness. If therefore the light that is in thee be darkness, how great is that darkness! No man can serve two masters: for either he will hate the one, and love the other; or else he will hold to the one, and despise the other. Ye cannot serve God and mammon.

Therefore I say unto you, Take no thought for your life, what ye shall eat, or what ye shall drink; nor yet for your body, what ye shall put on. Is not the life more than meat, and the body than raiment?

Behold the fowls of the air: for they sow not, neither do they reap, nor gather into barns; yet your heavenly Father feedeth them. Are ye not much better than they?

Which of you by taking thought can add one cubit to his stature?

And why take ye thought for raiment? Consider the lilies of the field, how they grow; they toil not, neither do they spin:

And yet I say unto you, That even Solomon in all his glory was not arrayed like one of these.

Wherefore, if God so clothe the grass of the field, which to day is, and to morrow is cast into the oven, shall he not much more clothe you, O ye of little faith?

Therefore take no thought, saying, What shall we eat? or, What shall we drink? or, Wherewithal shall we be clothed?

(For after all these things do the Gentiles seek:) for your heavenly Father knoweth that ye have need of all these things.

But seek ye first the kingdom of God, and his righteousness; and all these things shall be added unto you.

Take therefore no thought for the morrow: for the morrow shall take thought for the things of itself. Sufficient unto the day is the evil thereof. Judge not, that ye be not judged.

For with what judgement ye judge, ye shall be judged: and with what measure ye mete, it shall be measured to you again.

Give, and it shall be given unto you; good measure, pressed down, and shaken together, and running over, shall men give into your bosom.

And why beholdest thou the mote that is in thy brother's eye, but considerest not the beam that is in thine own eye?

Or how wilt thou say to thy brother, Let me pull out the mote out of thine eye; and, behold, a beam is in thine own eye?

Thou hypocrite, first cast out the beam out of thine own eye; and then shalt thou see clearly to cast out the mote out of thy brother's eye. Give not that which is holy unto the dogs, neither cast ye your pearls before swine, lest they trample them under their feet, and turn again and rend you.

Ask, and it shall be given you; seek, and ye shall find; knock, and it shall be opened unto you:

For every one that asketh receiveth; and he that seeketh findeth; and to him that knocketh it shall be opened.

Or what man is there of you, whom if his son ask bread, will he give him a stone? Or if he ask a fish, will he give him a serpent?

If ye then, being evil, know how to give good gifts unto your children, how much more shall your Father which is in heaven give good things to them that ask him?

Therefore all things whatsoever ye would that men should do to you, do ye even so to them: for this is the law and the prophets. Enter ye in at the strait gate: for wide is the gate, and broad is the way, that leadeth to destruction, and many there be which go in thereat:

Because strait is the gate, and narrow is the way, which leadeth unto life, and few there be that find it.

Beware of false prophets, which come to you in sheep's clothing, but inwardly they are ravening wolves.

Ye shall know them by their fruits. Do men gather grapes of thorns, or figs of thistles?

Even so every good tree bringeth forth good fruit; but a corrupt tree bringeth forth evil fruit.

A good tree cannot bring forth evil fruit, neither can a corrupt tree bring forth good fruit.

Every tree that bringeth not forth good fruit is hewn down, and cast into the fire. Wherefore by their fruits ye shall know them.

A good man out of the good treasure of the heart bringeth forth good things: and an evil man out of the evil treasure bringeth forth evil things.

But I say unto you, That every idle word that men shall speak, they shall give account thereof in the day of judgement.

For by thy words thou shalt be justified, and by thy words thou shalt be condemned. Therefore whosoever heareth these sayings of mine, and doeth them, I will liken him unto a wise man, which built his house upon a rock:

And the rain descended, and the floods came, and the winds blew, and beat upon that house; and it fell not: for it was founded upon a rock.

And every one that heareth these sayings of mine, and doeth them not, shall be likened unto a foolish man, which built his house upon the sand:

And the rain descended, and the floods came, and the
winds blew, and beat upon that house; and it fell: and great
was the fall of it.

From the Lord's Prayer, as it is, many fundamentals of
Christianity as practised are immediately visible—the belief in
one God who is our common Father; the fact that his abode
is heaven, and the promise that as God lives in bliss in heaven,
earth, in turn, will become like heaven. Resurrection of souls
that have lived on earth, who come back to earth, this time in
an immortal state, after a final Judgement Day, then follows.
Equally important is forgiveness of those who trespass
against us in order that we be forgiven for our own trespasses.
Importantly, one must be delivered from evil, otherwise one
will never attain this kingdom of heaven on earth.

Slowly and steadily the apostles swelled to twelve in
number and Jesus told them of the rewards of travelling all
over the country with him. 'He that findeth his life shall lose
it: and he that loseth his life for my sake shall find it' (KJV,
Matt. 10:39).

A parable likens the kingdom of heaven to a pearl of
great value found by a merchant who sold all his belongings
in order to purchase it. Jesus was given the power of
performing miracles and cured a number of persons
including a leper, Simon Peter's mother-in-law who was
sick with a fever, a palsied man and a paralytic. The story of
Jesus walking on water is also told, including the miracle of
feeding 5000 people without there being any food, the food
being provided by Jesus's prayer to God. It is Simon Peter

who first recognized that Jesus is the Messiah, the son of the living God. Jesus told him: 'That thou art Peter, and upon this rock I will build my church; and the gates of hell shall not prevail against it' (KJV, Matt. 16:18).

Another interesting event occurred when Jesus and his disciples were crossing the sea and a great storm arose. The disciples were frightened. But Jesus rebuked the wind, and said 'Peace be still' and the wind ceased and there was a great calm. And he said to his disciples, 'Why are you so fearful? How is it that ye have no faith?' This takes us to another very basic tenet of Christianity. The faith that one requires in order to be saved and live forevermore, owing to the grace of Jesus, the Christ.

On a mountain with Simon Peter, James and John, Jesus had a meeting with two Old Testament-prophets, Elijah and Moses. And a voice from a cloud said, this is my beloved Son. Jesus then charged these disciples that they should tell no man what they had seen until the Son of Man had risen from the dead.

Interesting parables are spoken of: like the one of the Good Samaritan and the one of the Prodigal Son. A lawyer asked for the meaning of one of the Ten Commandments; 'To love thy neighbour as thyself' was the answer given. He asked very pertinently as to who this neighbour was. To answer this question, Jesus told him a parable about a man who went away from Jerusalem to Jericho, was robbed by thieves, stripped and wounded, leaving him half dead. A Jewish priest and a Levite (Jew) passed, but did not stop.

A Samaritan (that is a person from a neighbouring land who was not a Jew) had compassion on him and took him to an inn, paying the innkeeper to care of him. Jesus asked, 'Which of these three men was his neighbour?' And the lawyer replied, 'He that showed mercy on him'. Jesus then told him, 'Go and do thou likewise'.

The other parable, 'The Prodigal Son', is about a man with two sons, the younger of whom asked for his inheritance, received it and wasted it, until he became penniless and was forced to labour as a swineherd. He decided to return to his father and asked to become one of his hired servants. The son told the father when he saw him that he had sinned against heaven, and was no more worthy to be called his son. But the father said to his servants, 'Bring forth the best robe, and put it on him; and put a ring on his hand, and shoes on his feet: And bring hither the fatted calf, and kill it; and let us eat, and be merry: For this my son was dead, and is alive again; he was lost, and is found. And they began to be merry.' The elder son was extremely angry at this behaviour of his father. He asked him as to why he favoured the younger son when everything that the elder son did was correct and everything that the younger son did was wrong. The answer he received was as follows: 'Son, thou art ever with me, and all that I have is thine. Your brother was dead, and is alive. He was lost and is now found. It is therefore meet that we should make merry.'

Yet another interesting event took place when Jesus went through Samaria on his way to Galilee. Wearied from his journey, he stopped on the way and requested a drink of water from a woman. Being a Samaritan, she asked Jesus how he would drink from her well as the Jews never drank water from a well used by the Samaritans. And Jesus answered her saying:

> If thou knewest the gift of God, and who it is that saith to thee, Give me to drink; thou wouldst have asked of him, and he would have given thee living water. Whosoever drinketh of this water shall thirst again: But whosoever drinketh of the water that I shall give him shall never thirst; but the water that I shall give him shall be in him a well of water springing up into everlasting life.

After the woman was amazed by Jesus's knowledge of the way in which she had lived life and sinned, Jesus went on to tell her that God is a Spirit, and they that worship Him must worship Him in Spirit and Truth. The woman went back to her city and told the people to come and see this great man who told her all these things. 'Is it not the Messiah?' she asked.

Once Jesus told his disciples:

> Ye seek me, not because ye saw the miracles, but because ye did eat of the loaves, and were filled. Labour not for the meat which perisheth, but for that meat which endureth unto everlasting life, which the Son of man shall give unto you . . . I am the bread of life: he that cometh to me shall never hunger; and he that believeth on me shall never thirst.

When a woman in danger was accused of being stoned to death for adultery, Jesus famously said to her accusers, 'Let him who has not sinned cast the first stone.' Jesus went on to liken himself to the good shepherd: 'I am the good shepherd: the good shepherd giveth his life for the sheep . . . And other sheep I have, which are not of this fold: them also I must bring, and they shall hear my voice; and there shall be one fold, and one shepherd.'

Another interesting thing that Jesus did was to bring a dead man back to life. A woman called Martha came to Jesus and said: 'My brother is dead but had you been there, he would not have died. But I know even now, whatever you will ask God, God will give it to you.' Jesus replied, 'Thy brother shall rise again. I am the resurrection and the life. He that believeth in me, though he were dead, yet shall he live and whosoever liveth and believeth in me shall never die.'

Finally, at the end of his ministry, Jesus rode triumphantly into Jerusalem on an ass and drove out of the temple money changers and those who transacted in money deals. When someone asked him to summarize the entire law in one sentence, he said, 'There are two commandments which all must follow. First, that thou shalt love the Lord thy God with all thy heart, and with all thy soul, and with all thy mind. And the second, that thou shalt love thy neighbour as thyself. On these two commandments hang all the law and the prophets.' Jesus then had the Last Supper with his disciples and said that the Son of Man will be betrayed to be crucified. Judas, one of the twelve apostles, betrayed him for thirty pieces of silver, and was later so ashamed that he hanged himself soon after.

Judas came with the Jewish priests to Gethsemane, where Jesus was, and in the morning, he was delivered to Pontius Pilate, the Roman governor of Judea. When Pontius Pilate asked him if he were king of the Jews, Jesus answered, 'It is you who are saying so.' When Pontius Pilate found that he had not transgressed the Roman law, he washed his hands off him and sent him to King Herod, who sent him back to Pilate, who then handed him over to the Jewish priests who demanded his crucifixion. The result was that the soldiers of Pontius Pilate took Jesus to Golgotha, on the outskirts of the city, and crucified him between two thieves. He was put up at nine in the morning and brought down at three in the afternoon, and put into a tomb nearby. On the third day, he rose from the dead and met Mary Magdalene and his disciples and told them to teach all nations, baptizing them in the name of the Father, the Son and the Holy Spirit.

Interestingly, the greatest and most zealous spreader of early Christianity was St Paul. St Paul had never seen Jesus in the flesh and was on his way to Damascus, busy persecuting Jesus's followers, when Jesus himself came to him as a spirit and admonished him saying, 'Saul, Saul, why does thou persecute me?' From that point on, Saul changed his name to Paul and went to countries outside Judea, preaching the Gospel of Jesus Christ. He wrote several epistles or letters to the various churches all over the region which form part of the New Testament canon. Indeed, the majority of the books of the New Testament consist of St Paul's teachings. Finally, St Peter and St Paul both landed up in Rome and were martyred to the cause of Jesus. After Jesus's death, seventy persons were sent out by Jesus, besides the immediate twelve apostles (Judas was replaced by Matthias), and they all went out to spread the gospel of Jesus the Christ.

After terrible persecutions, the Emperor Constantine promulgated an edict by which Christianity would now be tolerated throughout the Roman Empire. He personally called for the first Ecumenical Council at Nicaea in 325 CE where he wished to settle the controversial issue of the relationship between Jesus and God. Bishops from all over the Christian world came, and after several debates, what is called the Nicene Creed, which forms part of the central liturgy of the Roman Catholic Church, was drawn up. Everything hovered around one Greek word: *Homoousios* i.e., of the same substance, as opposed to *homoiousios*, which is of similar substance. The Nicene Creed settled for the first, proclaiming Jesus's divinity as God's only begotten son of the same substance as God the Father.

This creed, in turn, raised questions as to whether Jesus was wholly divine, and it is only in the fourth great council at Chalcedon, in 451 CE, that two natures of Christ were spoken of, and that Christ was, therefore, both human and divine—human and divine, not mixed together, but separate like oil and water. It is this version of Christ's divinity that has, through the centuries, finally emerged triumphant and is accepted by the Roman Catholic Church today.

The Roman Catholic Church is one of the few institutions that has existed for 2000 years, but there have been many breakaways. The first major breakaway took place in 1054 CE when the Eastern Orthodox churches, most notably Greek and Russian, broke away from Rome. Five hundred years later, in what would be called Protestantism, Martin Luther in Germany struck the first blow. At a church in Wittenberg, in 1517, Luther nailed what was called 95 Theses railing against the depravities of the then Pope Leo X and the Catholic Church in general. Luther wished to return to the simplicity of the early church making it clear that it is by divine grace and faith, on the basis of scripture, that men can attain salvation. Many other reformers then followed: Zwingli in Switzerland, Calvin in France and Jan Hus in Czechoslovakia, to name a few. A major breakaway from the Catholic Church was the Anglican Church, which was set up by Henry VIII of England, in 1534 CE, as the Pope did not grant Henry VIII a divorce from his first wife, Catherine of Aragon. The Anglican Church has since then had its own liturgy, prayer book, etc.

Many other Protestant denominations thereafter grew, particularly in the United States. There are the Methodists set up by a man called John Wesley; Pentecostalism which commemorates the descent of the Holy Spirit upon the followers of Jesus; the Quakers who are so called because they quake in the presence of God, also known as the Religious Society of Friends, founded by George Fox. There are Born Again Christians, Unitarians, and many evangelical churches all of which have broken from the Roman Catholic Church. Protestant churches reject the idea of a celibate priesthood and allow the clergy to marry. As a matter of fact, women have now become priests in the Anglican Church. The Protestant concept of God allows believers to use the power of reason so as to foster the development of both science and the arts. At the heart of Protestantism is hard work, frugality, discipline and a strong sense of responsibility. Ostentation of all kinds was and is rejected. Protestants also took the initiative in advocating religious freedom, which was enshrined in the very First Amendment to the Constitution of the United States.

Today there are over 900 million Protestants worldwide, out of two-and-a-half billion Christians. They therefore account for nearly 40 per cent of Christians worldwide. The basic teachings of Jesus, in essence, therefore, speak of Jesus dying on the cross in order to save mankind from the original sin of the first man, Adam, and it is by belief in this dogma, together with divine grace, that makes a person attain heaven. After Judgement Day, a final cut-off day, persons live here on Earth in a resurrected astral body for all time. Christianity believes in a heaven and a hell. Interestingly, it is a person's deeds that send him or her to hell but it is divine grace that sends him or her to heaven and eventually to Earth as a resurrected spirit. Hell is a place of torment, which may result in complete annihilation of the soul in the case of unrepentant sinners.

Islam

The central figure of Islam is Prophet Muhammed, who was born in Mecca in 570 CE and died in 632 CE. He is stated to be the last of all the prophets, numbering 313. 'Prophet' here is understood as a messenger, who has a message from God. Muhammed was a trader who received his first message from Archangel Gabriel at the age of forty, and these messages came down to him in the form of revelations, all of which were then compiled into one basic text, which was then called the Holy Quran. Muhammed was orphaned at the age of six and then brought up by his grandfather. He married a wealthy widow, Khadija, who was the first to know that he had received revelations and was the first to comfort him and tell him that these revelations were not hallucinations but were real. He encountered persecution as a result of which he had to leave Mecca for Medina in the year 622 CE. After several battles with the leading tribes from Mecca, he finally established his faith in Mecca before dying.

The Quran or the teachings which came down from Archangel Gabriel are contained in 114 *sura*s or chapters. The very opening chapter proclaims that this text is in the name of 'God, the All Merciful and the All Compassionate, Master of the Day of Judgement, You alone do we worship and from You alone do we seek help. Guide us to the straight path, the path of those You have favoured, not those who go astray.' The next chapter, entitled, 'The Cow', is considered a mini-Quran and gives us a good indication of the various pillars of the religion. It begins by stating that if you do not believe what is written in this book, produce one chapter or sura like it; and you will not be able to (Verses 23 and 24).

Verse 28 then tells us, 'You were dead and then Allah (God) gave you life, death again and then life again.' Allah created the Earth and seven heavens (Verse 29). Jews, Christians, Sabians (that is, those who lived in Yemen, and were monotheistic) and whoever believes in Allah and the Last Day (Judgement Day) and does good deeds, is a person who will attain God (Verse 62). Allah creates by the power of thought. Allah says 'Be' and it 'Becomes' (Verse 117). Muslims are told, fight those who fight against you but don't begin the fight. Allah dislikes aggressors—slay them only if attacked because persecution and disorder is worse than slaughter (Verses 190 and 191). You are also told that if they desist from fighting, don't fight against them, except against wrong-doers (Verse 193). Allah loves the charitable (Verse 195) and most importantly, there is no compulsion in religion (Verse 256).

In Chapter III of the Quran, titled, 'The family of Imran', Imran being the father of Mary, the mother of Jesus, we are told that both the Torah (the first five books of the

Old Testament) and the Gospels (the four synoptic Gospels) are revealed through Moses and Jesus, respectively, for mankind (Verse 3). We are then told how to read the Quran, some verses being allegorical and some being absolutely clear in meaning (Verse 7). The Quran then goes on to affirm and deny various tenets of Christianity as practised. It states that Jesus spoke from the very moment that he was born and was given birth by a virgin. He was given the power of performing miracles. In particular, he created a live bird from clay, he made the blind see, he healed a leper and he raised persons from the dead (Verses 46, 47 and 49). We are then told in unmistakable terms that there is no Trinity; God is One and Jesus is not a son of God (Chapter IV, Verse 171).

We are also told that Jesus himself is not God, as God has no partner (Chapter V, Verse 72). Jesus is a messenger, like other messengers sent before him; don't forget he is a human being—he has to eat food in order to exist (Chapter V, Verse 75). We are also told that Jesus did not die on the cross; a likeness of him was put up, and therefore it appeared as if he did (Chapter IV, Verse 157). The Quran then goes on to tell us that if God helps you, then none can overcome you and, conversely, if God forsakes you, nobody can help you (Chapter III, Verse 160). The world, it is stated, is transient— an enjoyment of delusion (Chapter III, Verse 185). Allah is All-hearing and All-seeing (Chapter IV, Verse 134).

We are reminded that no human being should be held in awe; no human being, only God (Chapter V, entitled 'The Table', Verse 44). Allah could have made mankind one community but chose not to, hence the diversity of men and faiths (Verse 48). In Chapter VI, entitled 'Cattle', we are told that on death, it is angels who lift the soul to take it to its next plane of existence (Verse 61). We are then told about the Devil. Incidentally, the Devil in Islam is a jinn, a spirit or a ghost and is not a fallen angel and is called Iblis. That Iblis is a *jinn*, as specifically stated in Chapter XVIII (called 'The Cave'), Verse 51. Chapter VII entitled the 'Heights' tells us, in Verses 11–18, how Iblis is in hell and will continue to be in hell till Judgement Day. When asked to prostrate before Adam, the first man, Iblis refused to do so, and pride therefore caused Iblis's fall. We are informed that till Muhammed, every nation on Earth has been sent a messenger from God in the chapter entitled 'Jonah' (Chapter X, Verse 47).

We are then told that messengers are sent as bearers of good tidings and to warn all the peoples of the world of the consequences of not following God's path (Chapter XVIII, Verse 57).

Importantly, we are told in Chapter XXII, entitled 'Pilgrimage' (Verse 78), that God has not ordained any hardship in religion. In Chapter XXIV, called 'Noor' or 'Light', God will ask you how long you were on Earth. The answer is only one day or part thereof. You are not created in vain (Verses 112–14). You are then told to repent for all the evil you have done, believe in God and do good work. It is then that Allah will transmute evil into Good (Chapter XXV, Verse 70). You are also told to be modest. Allah does not love those who boast. You are reminded that the harshest of all voices is that of the ass (Chapter XXXI, Verses 18 and 19).

One Allah day is a thousand days on Earth (Chapter XXXII, Verse 5). Allah created man by breathing His spirit into man (Verse 9). Hell is an abode where there is fire. Hell is there on Earth as well, which is a lower kind of punishment than the punishment after death (Verses 20 and 21). In Chapter XXXIII entitled 'Allies', we are informed that Mohammed, who has not fathered any son, is the seal (the last) of the prophets (Verse 40).

We are told that hypocrites will be punished appropriately (Chapter XXXIII, Verse 73). A description of Heaven is then given where there will be delicious fruits, cool drinks and *huri*s (Chapter XXXVIII, Verses 51 and 52). Those who believe, both men and women, go to heaven, their evil deeds being remitted by God (Chapter XLVIII, Verse 5). On the other hand, hypocrites and idolaters will find themselves in hell (Verse 6). Life on Earth is an illusion, full of play, idle talk, pageantry, boasting and rivalry (Chapter LVII, Verse 20). In Chapter LIX, entitled 'Gathering in Exile', Verse 23 tells us Allah's names: Knower of the Visible and the Invisible, Beneficent, Merciful, Sovereign Lord, Holy One, Peacekeeper, Keeper of the Faith, Guardian, Majestic, Compelling, Outstanding, One Who Creates Out of Nothing, Fashioner.

We are told that those who merely read scriptures, without understanding, and therefore do not practise what is stated in them, are like donkeys carrying a load of books—

they transport what they does not understand (Chapter LXII, Verse 5). We are told as to how Judgement Day will be heralded: there will be a trumpet which will give a blast after which the Earth and the mountains will get demolished in one crash. Heaven itself will split and eight angels will then uphold the throne of God (Chapter LXIX, Verses 13–17). Also, the sun will be overthrown, the stars will fall; wild beasts will herd together and the oceans will rise (Chapter LXXXI, entitled 'Cessation'). We are also told to place our faith not in this world but in the hereafter, for it is better and more lasting (Chapter LXXXVII, Verse 17). Finally, we are informed in Chapter CXII, entitled 'Unity', Verse 3, that God does not beget any son, nor was God Himself begotten.

The Islamic creed believes in six articles of faith: One God, Allah; angels who are created out of fire, who serve Allah; scriptures in the form of the Quran, which are revelations from above; prophets who are chosen by God to preach divine messages, Muhammed being the last of such prophets, with the last message to the last people who would be so warned; a belief in Judgement Day and a resurrection of all souls who will inhabit the Earth and live forever; and that everything good or bad is decreed by Almighty God. A Muslim is told that he has five duties—first of all to declare his faith, namely that there is One God, and that he believes in the message of Muhammed who is the messenger of God; pray five times every day; give alms—a mandatory 2.5 per cent of one's income per annum; fast during the holy month of Ramadan, which is when Prophet Muhammed first received his message; and at least once, in one's life, to

make a Haj pilgrimage—to go to Mecca to circumnavigate
the Kaaba, which is the holy of holies in Islam.

After Muhammed died, four family members followed
in quick succession. The first four Caliphs were: Abu Bakr,
his father-in-law; Umar, his father-in-law, who spread Islam
through North Africa and into Spain; Uthman, his son-in-
law, and Ali, his nephew and son-in-law. After Ali, Muawiyyah
started what is known as the Umayyad Caliphate, and it was
under Muawiyyah's son Yazid that the Battle of Karbala took
place in 680 CE in which Prophet Muhammed's grandson
Hussain and some of Hussains's children were slain. This led
to a schism, the schism being those who are Shias or belong to
the faction that broke off after the Battle of Karbala, to follow
in Prophet Muhammed's family's footsteps, the others being
referred to as Sunnis. Sunni literally means the people of the
Sunnah, that is the traditions of Prophet Muhammed and
form the majority of practising Muslims today. The Sunnis
believe in six major Hadith works, that is, commentaries on
the Quran and the life of Prophet Muhammed. They follow
four traditional schools of jurisprudence: Hanafi, Hanbali,
Maliki and Shafi'i. The Shia on the other hand have also
broken into many groups and are scattered all over the world,
the only Shia nation being Iran. Sufism or the mystic version
of persons who are born Muslims believe that one can reach
Allah through ecstasy and love—the greatest of them all being
Jalaluddin Rumi. The Mathnavi, a collection of his sayings in
poetical form, is ecstatic love for God.

Islam is a religion that monitors every aspect of one's
daily life as well; there are strict rules as to what one can

eat and what is forbidden food. Pork, carrion and blood are forbidden foods. Alcoholic drinks are prohibited, and a Muslim man is allowed to marry up to four women and is exhorted to treat them equally. He is told that however hard he tries, treating them equally will not be easy (Chapter IV, Verse 129). The basic idea was that from an unlimited number of wives, one could marry up to four wives so that outcasts such as widows and orphans are brought back into society. Islam, then, is the culmination of the Semitic religions beginning with Judaism, continuing with Christianity. It is a reaffirmation of both these faiths, correcting their aberrations while laying down a similar path for the Arab people to follow.

Sikhism

Sikhism is a relatively recent faith and was established by Guru Nanak in the fifteenth century. He was the first of ten gurus and came out with a message which was extremely important at that time and is equally important today—that Hindus and Muslims in India are equals. He journeyed to all parts of India. He actually visited Mecca with his Muslim friend Mardana. He spoke in temples and mosques. He was famous for having lain down with his feet facing the Kaaba. When he was alerted to the fact that his feet were pointing at the Kaaba and that he should immediately rise, he replied, 'Show me where God is not.' He spoke out against empty religious rituals and the caste system which was prevalent in India.

He was followed by the second guru, Guru Angad, who introduced the Gurmukhi script, the script in which the holy book of the Sikhs, the Guru Granth Sahib, is written. Sikhs are well known for their sense of charity, especially their *langar* which is free meals given to all persons without discrimination. This was started by Guru Nanak and continued by Guru Angad. The third guru, Guru Amar Das, railed against social inequalities and used the simple expedient of persons having their meals sitting together, whether they are of high or low caste. Importantly, he abolished the custom of *sati* in which a married woman was forced to burn herself on the funeral pyre of her dead husband. *Purdah* or the veil was also done away with by this guru.

The fourth, Guru Ram Das, began the construction of the famous Golden Temple at Amritsar. Importantly, he requested a Sufi saint, Mian Mir, to lay the foundation stone of the Harmandir Sahib (temple to God) in the Golden Temple. The temple is open on all sides and at all times to everyone, as the Sikhs believe that the one God who is the Creator of all will be open to worship by all people at any time and from anywhere.

The next guru, Guru Arjan Dev, was instrumental in compiling the Guru Granth Sahib. He became the first great martyr in Sikh history when the Mughal Emperor Jahangir ordered his execution. With his execution, his son, Guru Har Gobind, was the first guru to become a rebel, organizing an army. He established the principles of *miri* and *piri*, representing temporal and spiritual power. He took up the sword in order to protect his weak and oppressed flock. It is this guru who erected the Akal Takht (the Throne of God, the Timeless One), an important building opposite the Harmandir Sahib in the Golden Temple.

Upon his death, his grandson, Guru Har Rai, a child guru at the age of fourteen, continued the work of his grandfather. When he died, his son, Guru Har Krishan, became the next guru. He was precocious from the beginning. Astonishing people with his wealth of knowledge, the young guru attended to sufferers from disease and unfortunately caught smallpox and died at the age of seven. At the time of his death, his great uncle, Guru Tegh Bahadur, became the ninth guru, being a younger son of the sixth guru, Guru Har Gobind. He was a great martyr of Sikhism in that he was ordered to be executed for not converting to Islam as he took it upon himself to challenge the Mughal Emperor Aurangzeb for attempting to forcibly convert some Kashmiri Pandits.

On his death, Gobind Singh became the tenth and last guru. Guru Gobind Singh created a group of five pure persons called the Khalsa—so-called because they were ready to give up their lives, believing they would be slaughtered. Every time the guru's bloodstained sword appeared, after a predecessor had supposedly been killed, the next person followed to what was expected to be certain death. Every time the guru had dipped his sword in the blood of an animal who had been slaughtered. These persons were therefore administered *amrit*, or the nectar of immortality which they had earned. The tradition of the Khalsa consists of the five Ks: *kesh*, or uncut hair; *kangha*, a wooden comb; *kara*, a steel bangle; *kirpan*, a sword; and *kaccha*, or shorts. This great guru fought many battles against the Mughal emperor Aurangzeb, and lost his father, mother and four sons to Aurangzeb's wrath. He was famous for having written a defiant letter to the Mughal emperor in which he predicted the downfall of the Mughal empire. Finally, he died at Nanded where he proclaimed that from then on there would be no human guru. From then on, the Guru Granth Sahib would be treated as the only guru of the Sikhs for all time.

The Guru Granth Sahib is a compilation of verses of six of the gurus: the first five, and the ninth, Guru Tegh Bahadur. In addition, other contributors included Hindu *bhakt*s and Sufi saints. A major share of contribution goes to the great Indian Bhakti saint Kabir, other contributors being Ravidas, Farid, Surdas and Jaidev, to mention a few. In addition, many Hindu Saraswat Brahmins who converted to Sikhism also contributed, most notable among them being Bhatt Kalshar, Bhatt Jalap and Bhatt Mathur.

The Guru Granth Sahib begins by invoking the name of Almighty God as 'Ek Onkar Sat Nam', which means 'One God is Eternal Truth'. This is followed by the Sikh's most holy prayer, called the 'Japji', composed by Guru Nanak. The Japji, which is also referred to as a mini Guru Granth Sahib, begins by stating that outward cleanliness and outward silence do not lead to God, as cleanliness and silence must come from within. This is based on the realization that it is by God's command that both happiness and suffering are given to mankind. It is God alone who relieves all living beings from the cycles of rebirth. The best way, therefore, is to constantly think of God, sing His name and love Him as all living beings abide in Him. God is formless and indescribable. He watches over all, even though none can see

Him. God alone is the primal one, the pure light without a beginning, without an end, and never changing.

The message of the Guru Granth Sahib can be summarized by stating that equality of mankind and womankind is the cardinal principle of this faith, and belief in One Creator, God, who looks after all living beings. It is important to speak and live truthfully. It is equally important to control the five vices, which are stated to be pride, anger, greed, lust and desire. One way of controlling these is to live in contentment and to inculcate a positive attitude to life. Humility, kindness, compassion and love to all human beings is basic to Sikhism. We are told that if these are not practised, the ghost within our skeleton turns to dry wood. And when the messenger of death grabs us by our hair, we will be punished by having fallen into death's mouth.

The Bahai Faith

One Sayyid Qasim spoke of two persons who will come to preach the Gospel of God. Sayid Qasim, after making this statement, died in 1843. One Mulla Husayn, his disciple, goes to find these two people. In a visit to the city of Shiraz in Persia, he finds a man called Ali Muhammad who is a Sayyid, known by his green turban, i.e., a descendant of the Prophet Muhammad. This person is referred to as 'the Bab', which means the gate of God, as he is to proclaim that a person greater than him is to come and actually deliver a message from God. He prophesied that he will be killed in ushering in this new prophet: the new prophet is the one who will make God manifest.

In 1844, the Bab goes to Mecca and Medina and looks out for the new prophet. One Mirza Husayn Ali, aged twenty-seven, becomes his follower. The Mirza was born to a wealthy and influential family and showed great spiritual wisdom as a child, being fully versed with the problems of humanity. He showed great love and compassion for the poor, apart from being an intellectually gifted person.

The Bab, as predicted, lasted for about six years, after which he was ordered to be executed. It is said that an

Armenian regiment of some 250 soldiers fired at him and another young man. The young man escaped unhurt, whereas the Bab disappeared. He was shot at again after being found in his cell, and this time executed successfully. This happened on 9 July 1845. Meanwhile, his follower, Mirza Husayn Ali, was put into a dungeon, and was able to escape to the city of Baghdad in 1853.

On 15 April 1854, the Mirza went into seclusion in a cave and emerged after two years. He turned out to be a versatile writer who wrote prolifically in both Persian and Arabic. In an early work called *The Hidden Words*, man is referred to as a spiritual being. Two of his early followers, one Ismael and one Mulla Muhammad, were struck by the wisdom of his utterances. He then penned what is known as the *Kitab-i-Iqaan* or the *Book of Certitude*, written with lightning speed in just two days, to answer four questions posed by the Bab's maternal uncle. He declared himself Bahaulla or the Glory of God in 1863, when visiting Constantinople, after which he then went to Adrianople. From there he sent letters to kings and leaders all over the world, including the Shah of Persia the Uthman Sultan, Napoleon III, the Kaiser of Germany, the Tsar in Russia, Queen Victoria in England and Pope Pius XIX. After spending five years in Adrianople, he went to Cyprus in 1868, and then to Akka where he spent twenty-four years, mostly in imprisonment.

There, among other treatises, he wrote the single-most important book in Bahai religious literature, the *Kitab-i-Aqdas*, which means the Most Holy Book, written in

Arabic. He was known to dictate books to many secretaries at lightning speed. And he spoke repeatedly of One God, who is different from his creation, but who is mirrored in human beings. He spoke of progressive revelations through time beginning with Zarathustra, continuing with Lord Krishna, the Buddha, Jesus and other great prophets. He went on to state that if contradictory messages were given by all these great prophets, it was only due to the manner in which the followers of these prophets misunderstood their teaching, which were all similar.

He said repeatedly that God creates us from love and the world beyond Him is as different as the world is for a child that lives in the womb as compared to a child after its birth. Death is said to be a messenger of joy because the soul will then progress until it reaches the presence of Almighty God. Interestingly, we are told that both heaven and hell exist, heaven being nearness to God and hell being remoteness from God. We are told to be pure and upright and, in the words of the *Gleanings*, another one of the books dictated by Bahaulla:

Be generous in prosperity, and thankful in adversity. Be worthy of the trust of thy neighbour, and look upon him with a bright and friendly face. Be a treasure to the poor, an admonisher to the rich, an answerer to the cry of the needy, a preserver of the sanctity of thy pledge. Be fair in thy judgement, and guarded in thy speech. Be unjust to no man, and show all meekness to all men. Be as a lamp unto them that walk in darkness, a joy to the sorrowful, a sea for the thirsty, a haven for the distressed, an upholder and defender of the victim of oppression. Let integrity and uprightness distinguish all thine acts. Be a home for the stranger, a balm to the suffering, a tower of strength for the fugitive. Be eyes to the blind, and a guiding light unto the feet of the erring. Be an ornament to the countenance of truth, a crown to the brow of fidelity, a pillar of the temple of righteousness, a breath of life to the body of mankind, an ensign of the hosts of justice, a luminary above the horizon of virtue, a dew to the soil of the human heart, an ark on the ocean of knowledge, a sun in the heaven of bounty, a gem on the diadem of wisdom, a shining light in the firmament of thy generation, a fruit upon the tree of humility.

We are also told that justice is best loved by God as there will be reward and punishment for every deed; therefore, love and fear God equally. Bahaulla made as many as four trips to Haifa and there wrote a *Tablet of Carmel* and the *Epistle to the Son of the Wolf.* In 1892, just as he was freed from prison, he died. In the *Book of the Covenant*, he spoke of the greater and the lesser, the greater being the prophets of Almighty God and the lesser being Bahaulla himself, stating that no schisms must occur after his advent. He then appointed his son, Abdul Baha, before he died, to be his successor. Abdul Baha, in turn, died in 1921, appointing his eldest son, Shoghi Effendi, to lead the Bahais.

Many Bahai teachings speak of the importance of prayer, the unity of God and the importance of following God's commandments. Eighteen days of fasting are enjoined upon every Bahai from 2 to 20 March, after which the great festival of Navroz, on the 21 of March, is then celebrated by feasting. Bahaulla preached that just as there is One God, there should be one religion, one humanity, one language and complete equality of the sexes. Science and religion are not antithetical to each other, and are to be harmonized by independent investigations of the truth. Both extreme wealth and extreme poverty are bad and should be eliminated, as moderation in living is stressed upon. Celibacy is frowned upon as it is important to marry and bring up a family. Alcohol and drugs are prohibited, whereas music is encouraged as it is the food of love. All tests and afflictions in this life are only in order to make mankind ready for the life to come. Interestingly, evil is described not as a force by itself but as the absence of good, which is as a result of the lower nature of man.

Kitab-i-Aqdas

The *Kitab-i-Aqdas*, or the Most Holy Book, discusses many subjects, both metaphysical and ethical. It begins with a proclamation of the recognition of the manifestation of God through his revelations to Bahaulla for this particular age, and the obedience to his laws. It also has an interesting passage on 'notions of liberty', pejoratively speaking, as meaning a licence to disregard God's law. Bahaulla speaks of how he's going to appoint one of his sons as his successor.

A 'guardianship' is also spoken of by which his descendants will look after the administration of charitable endowments. He tells the Bahais to establish a House of Justice in each city where there are at least nine believers. The House of Justice seems to refer to a council which is a sort of Supreme Authority over the Bahai community. He then speaks about religious tax which is a major source of revenue for the upkeep of the Universal House of Justice.

When it comes to religious practices, obligatory prayers and fasting are commended in this book. It also speaks of pilgrimage, communal morning prayers, funereal laws and Bahai holy days. It deals in detail with subjects such as marriage, divorce and inheritance, and speaks of punishments for the crimes of murder, arson, theft and adultery. Many of these laws abrogate early laws, which have outlived their utility. Muttering prayers in the streets, destroying books, kissing hands as a sign of respect are all outlawed.

Ethical principles are then spoken of in general rather than in particular terms. Virtues such as truthfulness, courteousness, tact, perseverance are all stressed. Above all, music and its benefits are extolled. A general life of moderation and temperance is extolled. The book also advocates tolerance; that it is important to show friendship to those who believe in other religions; that children should be educated, and that everybody should be usefully occupied in lawful professions. Many other passages which speak to rulers all over the world include prophecies that are made: the fall of Istanbul, that the banks of the Rhine will be covered with blood, that this will occur twice (referring to the two World Wars), and the lamentations of Berlin will then be heard.

Passages from this book are interesting and set out the principles of the Bahai faith. It is stated:

> Oh peoples of the world! Know assuredly that My commandments are the lamps of My loving providence among My servants, and the keys of My mercy for My creatures. Thus hath it been sent down from the heaven of the Will of your Lord, the Lord of Revelation. Were any man to taste the sweetness of the words which the lips of the All-Merciful have willed to utter, he would, though the treasures of the earth be in his possession, renounce them one and all, that he might vindicate the truth of even one of His commandments, shining above the Dayspring of His bountiful care and loving-kindness.

And then again, these are the ordinances of God that have been set down in His tablets and statutes by His most exalted pen:

> Hold ye fast unto His statutes and commandments, and be not of those who, following their idle fancies and vain imaginings, have clung to the standards fixed by their own selves, and cast behind their backs the standards laid down by God. Abstain from food and drink from sunrise to sundown, and beware lest desire deprive you of this grace that is appointed in the Book.

Ye have been forbidden to commit murder or adultery, or to engage in backbiting or calumny; shun ye, then, what hath been prohibited in the holy Books and Tablets.

O people of Baha! It is incumbent upon each one of you to engage in some occupation—such as a craft, a trade or the like. We have exalted your engagement in such work to the rank of worship of the one true God. Reflect, O people, on the grace and blessings of your Lord, and yield Him thanks at eventide and dawn. Waste not your hours in idleness and sloth, but occupy yourselves with what will profit you and others. Thus hath it been decreed in this Tablet from whose horizon hath shone the daystar of wisdom and utterance. The most despised of men in the sight of God are they who sit and beg. Hold ye fast unto the cord of means and place your trust in God, the Provider of all means.

Say: Rejoice not in the things ye possess; tonight they are yours, tomorrow others will possess them. Thus warneth you He Who is the All-Knowing, the All-Informed. Say: Can ye claim that what ye own is lasting or secure? Nay! By Myself, the All-Merciful, ye cannot, if ye be of them who judge fairly. The days of your life flee away as a breath of wind, and all your pomp and glory shall be folded up as were the pomp and glory of those gone before you. Reflect, O people! What hath become of your bygone days, your lost centuries? Happy the days that have been consecrated to the remembrance of God, and blessed the hours which have been spent in praise of Him Who is the All-Wise. By My life! Neither the pomp of the mighty, nor the wealth of the rich, nor even the ascendancy of the ungodly will endure. All will perish, at a word from Him. He, verily, is the All-Powerful, the All-Compelling, the Almighty. What advantage is there in the earthly things which men possess? That which shall profit them, they have utterly neglected. Erelong, they will awake from their slumber, and find themselves unable to obtain that which hath escaped them in the days of their Lord, the Almighty, the All-Praised. Did they but know it, they would renounce their all, that their names may be mentioned before His throne. They, verily, are accounted among the dead.

Unto every father hath been enjoined the instruction of his son and daughter in the art of reading and writing and in all that hath been laid down in the Holy Tablet. He that putteth away that which is commanded unto him, the Trustees are then to take from him that which is required for their instruction if he be wealthy and, if not, the matter devolveth upon the House of Justice. Verily have We made it a shelter for the poor and needy. He that bringeth up his son or the son of another, it is as though he hath brought up a son of Mine; upon him rest My glory, My loving-kindness, My mercy, that have compassed the world.

It is forbidden you to trade in slaves, be they men or women. It is not for him who is himself a servant to buy another of God's servants, and this hath been prohibited in His Holy Tablet. Thus, by His mercy, hath the commandment been recorded by the Pen of justice. Let no man exalt himself above another; all are but bondslaves before the Lord, and all exemplify the truth that there is none other God but Him. He, verily, is the All-Wise, Whose wisdom encompasseth all things.

O kings of the earth! He Who is the sovereign Lord of all is come. The Kingdom is God's, the omnipotent Protector, the Self-Subsisting. Worship none but God, and, with radiant hearts, lift up your faces unto your Lord, the Lord of all names. This is a Revelation to which whatever ye possess can never be compared, could ye but know it.

Resort ye, in times of sickness, to competent physicians; We have not set aside the use of material means, rather have We confirmed it through this Pen, which God hath made to be the Dawning-place of His shining and glorious Cause.

And then the delightful passage on liberty:

Consider the pettiness of men's minds. They ask for that which injureth them, and cast away the thing that profiteth them. They are, indeed, of those that are far astray. We find some men desiring liberty, and priding themselves therein. Such men are in the depths of ignorance.

Liberty must, in the end, lead to sedition, whose flames none can quench. Thus warneth you He Who is the Reckoner, the All-Knowing. Know ye that the embodiment of liberty and its symbol is the animal. That which beseemeth man is submission unto such restraints as will protect him from his own ignorance, and guard him against the harm of the mischief maker. Liberty causeth man to overstep the bounds of propriety, and to infringe on the dignity of his station. It debaseth him to the level of extreme depravity and wickedness.

Regard men as a flock of sheep that need a shepherd for their protection. This, verily, is the truth, the certain truth. We approve of liberty in certain circumstances, and refuse to sanction it in others. We, verily, are the All-Knowing.

Say: True liberty consisteth in man's submission unto My commandments, little as ye know it. Were men to observe that which We have sent down unto them from the Heaven of Revelation, they would, of a certainty, attain unto perfect liberty. Happy is the man that hath apprehended the Purpose of God in whatever He hath revealed from the Heaven of His Will that pervadeth all created things. Say: The liberty that profiteth you is to be found nowhere except in complete servitude unto God, the Eternal Truth. Whoso hath tasted of its sweetness will refuse to barter it for all the dominion of earth and heaven.

Consort with all religions with amity and concord, that they may inhale from you the sweet fragrance of God. Beware lest amidst men the flame of foolish ignorance overpower you. All things proceed from God and unto Him they return. He is the source of all things and in Him all things are ended.

Ye have been forbidden in the Book of God to engage in contention and conflict, to strike another, or to commit similar acts whereby hearts and souls may be saddened. A fine of nineteen mithqáls of gold had formerly been prescribed by Him Who is the Lord of all mankind for anyone who was the cause of sadness to another; in this Dispensation, however, He hath absolved you thereof and exhorteth you to show forth righteousness and piety. Such is the commandment which He hath enjoined upon you in this resplendent Tablet. Wish not for others what ye wish not for yourselves; fear God and be not of the prideful. Ye are all created out of water, and unto dust shall ye return. Reflect upon the end that awaiteth you and walk not in the ways of the oppressor. Give ear unto the verses of God which He Who is the sacred Lote-Tree reciteth unto you. They are assuredly the infallible balance, established by God, the Lord of this world and the next. Through them the soul of man is caused to wing its flight towards the Dayspring of Revelation, and the heart of every true believer is suffused with light. Such are the laws which God hath enjoined upon you, such His commandments prescribed unto you in His Holy Tablet; obey them with joy and gladness, for this is best for you, did ye but know.

Recite ye the verses of God every morn and eventide. Whoso faileth to recite them hath not been faithful to the

Covenant of God and His Testament, and whoso turneth away from these holy verses in this Day is of those who throughout eternity have turned away from God. Fear ye God, O My servants, one and all. Pride not yourselves on much reading of the verses or on a multitude of pious acts by night and day; for were a man to read a single verse with joy and radiance it would be better for him than to read with lassitude all the Holy Books of God, the Help in Peril, the Self-Subsisting. Read ye the sacred verses in such measure that ye be not overcome by languor and despondency. Lay not upon your souls that which will weary them and weigh them down, but rather what will lighten and uplift them, so that they may soar on the wings of the Divine verses towards the Dawning-place of His manifest signs; this will draw you nearer to God, did ye but comprehend.

Were He to decree as lawful the thing which from time immemorial had been forbidden, and forbid that which had, at all times, been regarded as lawful, to none is given the right to question His authority. Whoso will hesitate, though it be for less than a moment, should be regarded as a transgressor.

Immerse yourselves in the ocean of My words, that ye may unravel its secrets, and discover all the pearls of wisdom that lie hid in its depths. Take heed that ye do not vacillate in your determination to embrace the truth of this Cause—a Cause through which the potentialities of the might of God have been revealed, and His sovereignty established. With faces beaming with joy, hasten ye unto Him. This is the changeless

Faith of God, eternal in the past, eternal in the future. Let him that seeketh, attain it; and as to him that hath refused to seek it—verily, God is Self-Sufficient, above any need of His creatures.

This is a Book which hath become the Lamp of the Eternal unto the world, and His straight, undeviating Path amidst the peoples of the earth. Say: This is the Dayspring of Divine knowledge, if ye be of them that understand, and the Dawning-place of God's commandments, if ye be of those who comprehend.

The *Kitab-i-Iqaan* or the Book of Certitude, as has been stated earlier, was composed in two days and nights and was a reply to four questions asked by the Bab's maternal uncle. The book is in two parts. The first part states that divine revelation is progressive, and all religions are related to one another, with each monotheistic faith accepting the previous one and prophesying the advent of the next one, albeit in veiled terms. The second and larger part of the book is a discourse on the mission of the Bab which contains the famous passage entitled 'The Passage of the True Seeker'. Shoghi Effendi, the then leader of the faith, has summarized the contents of this remarkable book as follows:

Within a compass of two hundred pages it proclaims unequivocally the existence and oneness of a personal God,

unknowable, inaccessible, the source of all Revelation,
eternal, omniscient, omnipresent and almighty; asserts
the relativity of religious truth and the continuity of
Divine Revelation; affirms the unity of the Prophets,
the universality of their Message, the identity of their
fundamental teachings, the sanctity of their scriptures,
and the twofold character of their stations; denounces
the blindness and perversity of the divines and doctors
of every age; cites and elucidates the allegorical passages
of the New Testament, the abstruse verses of the Quran,
and the cryptic Muhammadan traditions which have bred
those age-long misunderstandings, doubts and animosities
that have sundered and kept apart the followers of the
world's leading religious systems; enumerates the essential
prerequisites for the attainment by every true seeker of the
object of his quest; demonstrates the validity, the sublimity
and significance of the Bab's Revelation; acclaims the
heroism and detachment of His disciples; foreshadows,
and prophesies the world-wide triumph of the Revelation
promised to the people of the Bayan; upholds the purity
and innocence of the Virgin Mary; glorifies the Imams
of the Faith of Muhammad; celebrates the martyrdom,
and lauds the spiritual sovereignty, of the Imam Husayn;
unfolds the meaning of such symbolic terms as 'Return,'
'Resurrection,' 'Seal of the Prophets' and 'Day of
Judgment'; adumbrates and distinguishes between the
three stages of Divine Revelation; and expatiates, in
glowing terms, upon the glories and wonders of the 'City

of God,' renewed, at fixed intervals, by the dispensation of Providence, for the guidance, the benefit and salvation of all mankind. Well may it be claimed that of all the books revealed by the Author of the Bahai Revelation, this Book alone, by sweeping away the age-long barriers that have so insurmountably separated the great religions of the world, has laid down a broad and unassailable foundation for the complete and permanent reconciliation of their followers.

Part I of this book begins by saying that if we can follow the path of faith, and thirst for the wine of certitude, then we must first cleanse yourself from all that is earthly: that is idle talk, vain imagining, worldly affections and love of that which perishes. Trust only in God. All the prophets that have come are awaited by mankind with bated breath. And these prophets also speak of those who will follow them. Yet when they actually come, they are reviled by mankind. Examples are then given of those prophets who were reviled: Noah, Hud, Saleh, a prophet called the Friend of God, Moses, Jesus, who specifically states that 'I will go and then return. Another will also come to tell you things that I have not yet told', and Muhammad who says that 'I am Jesus and all the prophets'.

The so-called leaders of every religion really hinder the path to salvation, owing to their lust for power. Many sayings of the prophets are then explained. Jesus said that when oppression comes, he will return. 'Oppression' really means a soul who seeks the truth but does not know where to go. The sun, the moon and the stars collapsing means that the prophets, the saints, their laws and their teachings will all amount to nought. The sun and the moon falling down speaks of the twin religious precepts of fasting and prayer disappearing; 'the cleaving of heaven' refers to divine revelation that comes from heaven being annulled by humanity.

Knowledge is of two kinds: divine and satanic. God teaches divine knowledge, which comes with patience, understanding and love. Satanic knowledge consists of arrogance, vanity and conceit. 'The clouds of heaven' spoken of by the prophets speak of dark clouds that will obscure and obstruct the knowledge of God. In today's world, the Jews pervert the text of the Pentateuch, just as the Muslims pervert the text of the Holy Quran. The followers of Bahaulla are told that there is no great piety in turning east or west and then praying. Piety consists only in believing in God and in the last day or Judgement Day.

Part II of the book then speaks of how all the prophets have come down with the same message, revealing Almighty God's attributes. Life is said to culminate in faith, at which point life knows no death and becomes everlasting. Death is only of those who do not believe. An interesting story is told of one Sadiq, who tells a poor man that he has all the wealth of the world. The poor man says, 'I'm destitute.' Sadiq says, 'Do you not have my love?' The poor man has to agree. He also agrees that he will not exchange this love, even for 1000 dinars (which is a fortune). Ultimately, we are taught that the only wealth is God and the only poverty is the lack of understanding that God alone is the be all and end all of everything.

Bahaulla then goes on to state that the true meaning of Muhammad being 'the seal' of the prophets, is twisted by the Muslims. Muhammad says: 'I am all the prophets; I am the first and the last.' It is in this sense that the word 'seal' is used, not in the sense of being the last after which there will be no other prophet, because the Quran itself says God doeth as he pleaseth and the ultimate interpretation of 'seal of the prophets' is with God.

Part II contains a beautiful summation of Bahaulla's teachings:

The seeker should regard backbiting as grievous error, and keep himself aloof from it, inasmuch as backbiting quencheth the light of the heart, and extinguisheth the life of the soul. He should be content with little, and be freed from all inordinate desire. He should treasure the companionship of those that have renounced the world, and regard avoidance of boastful and worldly people. At the dawn of every day he should commune with God, and with all his soul persevere in the quest of his Beloved. He should consume every wayward thought with the flame of His loving mention, and, with the swiftness of lightning, pass by all else save Him. He should succour the dispossessed, and never withhold his favour from the destitute. He should show kindness to animals, and more unto his fellowman, to him who is endowed with the power of utterance. He should not hesitate to offer up his life for his Beloved, nor allow the censure of the people to turn him away from the Truth. He should not wish for others that which he doth not wish for himself, nor promise that which he doth not fulfil. With all his heart should the seeker avoid fellowship with evildoers, and pray for the remission of their sins. He should forgive the sinful, and never despise his low estate, for none knoweth what his own end shall be. How often hath a sinner, at the hour of death, attained to the essence of faith, and, quaffing the immortal draft, hath taken his flight unto the celestial Concourse. And how often hath a devout believer, at the hour of his soul's ascension, been so changed as to fall into the nethermost fire. Our purpose in revealing these convincing and weighty utterances is to impress upon the seeker that he should regard all else beside God as transient, and count all things save Him, Who is the Object of all adoration, as utter nothingness.

These are among the attributes of the exalted and constitute the hallmark of the spiritually minded. They have already been mentioned in connection with the requirements of the wayfarers that tread the Path of Positive Knowledge. When the detached wayfarer and sincere seeker hath fulfilled these essential conditions, then and only then can he be called a true seeker. Whensoever he hath fulfilled the conditions implied in the verse: 'Whoso maketh efforts for Us, he shall enjoy the blessing conferred by the words, In Our ways shall We assuredly guide him.' Only when the lamp of search, of earnest striving, of longing desire, of passionate devotion, of fervid love, of rapture, and ecstasy, is kindled within the seeker's heart, and the breeze of His loving-kindness is wafted upon his soul, will the darkness of error be dispelled, the mists of doubts and misgivings be dissipated, and the lights of knowledge and certitude envelop his being. At that hour will the mystic Herald, bearing the joyful tidings of the Spirit, shine forth from the City of God resplendent as the morn, and, through the trumpet-blast of knowledge, will awaken the heart, the soul, and the spirit from the slumber of negligence. Then will the manifold favours and outpouring grace of the holy and everlasting Spirit confer such new life upon the seeker that he will find himself endowed with a new eye, a new ear, a new heart, and a new mind. He will contemplate the manifest signs of the Universe, and will penetrate the hidden mysteries of the soul. Gazing with the eye of God, he will perceive within every atom a door that leadeth him to the stations of absolute certitude. He will discover in all things the mysteries of divine Revelation.

The book then ends stating that whosoever shall withdraw from the remembrance of the Merciful, we shall chain a Satan unto him and He shall be his fast companion.

Part II: The Non-Theistic Faiths

Jainism

Jainism is one of the oldest religions of this world and is essentially atheistic as it believes in a Universe which is eternal, and with what it calls *jivas* or floating spirits, which also are eternal. It believes that when these jivas come into contact with matter, they get trapped within a cycle of transmigration. One can transmigrate upwards from an amoeba right up to a human being; that it can take 84,00,000 lives for a particular living being to move upwards to being human in this way. The moving upwards, of course, is policed by the doctrine of karma, which then assigns the true place in this ladder of transmigration to every jiva as soon as it perishes.

The founder of Jainism was a man called Rishabhanatha, who lived in hoary antiquity. He is considered as the first of twenty-four Tirthankaras or persons who have crossed the bridge so as to leave behind the world of transmigration and attain what is called nirvana or their own pristine jiva in its original, uncontaminated state. The first Tirthankara and twenty-three others who follow him are all such persons whose lives and teaching ought therefore to be emulated. The last three Tirthankaras namely, Neminatha, Pashvanatha, who is said to have existed some time in the eighth century BCE, and Mahavira, who is said to have existed in the sixth century BCE, are all historical personages.

Vardhaman Mahavira, the twenty-fourth, apparently left home at the age of twenty-eight and led a life of extreme austerity for twelve years. At the end of the twelfth year, he attained what is called *kevalgyan,* or omniscience, and was given the title Mahavira or a great, brave man. He spent thirty years of his life teaching this religious system and organizing his order of ascetics. Mahavira's followers were drawn chiefly from the Kshatriya *varna,* that is the varna of warriors.

A great schism occurred in his followers which took place in 79 CE dividing them into what is called Shwetambara or white-robed, and Digambara or sky-clad/nude. These sects are further subdivided into various subsects, some of which do not believe in idol worship. Jainism believes in six *dravya*s or substances. The first dravya or substance is, as has been stated, a jiva or a spirit. The *ajiva* dravyas or those that are not spirit are stated first to be *pudgal,* which is matter; *dharma,* which is motion; *adharma,* which is rest; *kala,* which is time; and *aakash,* which is space. Pudgal consists of atoms which can be solid, liquid or in the air.

Jainism also believes in what are called seven *tattvas,* or principles. The first is the spirit, jiva; the second is ajiva or matter; the third is *asrava,* which is inflow; the fourth is *bandh,* or bondage; the fifth is *samvad,* which is to check the inflow; the sixth is *nirjara,* which is the ability to shed previous karma; and the seventh is *moksha* or final liberation. Each jiva is divided into 406 types, depending on the number of senses that it may or may not contain and depending upon whether it is on Earth or elsewhere. Jivas which have one sense such as Earth, Water, Fire, etc., are said to be eighty-one in number. Likewise, jivas going up to five senses which are not human are said to be of forty-two types. Jivas in humans are supposed to be of thirteen types. Jivas, which are in the celestial regions—that is, in sixteen heavens—are 172 types, and those that are in the lower regions are ninety-eight types. It is these jivas, along with certain inanimate objects like water courses, that transmigrate throughout these regions.

There are also stated to be jivas that are perfect (*nityasiddha*), *mukta* (liberated) and *baddha* (bound). The doctrine of karma is what governs a jiva and then produces, therefore, either painful or pleasant consequences. When a particular karma produces good, it will purge bad karma and finally, depending upon the good and evil that has been done by a particular jiva, it will go either to hell, to the animal world, into human society or to the heavens.

Jainism claims that there is no Creator God necessary for creation. It is stated that there can be no destruction of things that do exist nor can there be creation of things out of nothing coming into existence and then ceasing to exist. Things have only their attributes. There is no need to assume any first cause of the Universe. We cannot conceive how a non-creative God suddenly becomes creative. Did God create something out of nothing? Since that is not possible, obviously God created something out of something which must have existed eternally. Importantly, it is argued that everything that exists must have a maker in which case the maker himself would stand in need of another maker which would lead to an infinite number of makers. The best way to escape from such a circle is therefore to assume the reality of the Universe existing by itself. The whole Universe consisting of spiritual and material factors has, therefore, existed from all eternity, undergoing an infinite number of incarnations.

Importantly, the Jains do not hold that everything is momentary; they hold that what is permanent is the basic substance of a thing consisting of atoms and what is liable to change is that which manifests itself and may be defaced or may die, depending upon whether it is inanimate or animate.

A Jain monk is supposed to take five vows. The first is *ahimsa,* the single-most important principle in Jainism, which is non-injury to any living being. This is taken to great lengths. The reason why Jains do not eat either onions or garlic is because they grow under the ground, and in attempting to remove onions or garlic from the ground, one may kill insects. The second is *satya*, or truth. The third is *asteya*, or non-stealing. The fourth is *aparigraha*, or the absence of desire, and the fifth is *brahmacharya*, which apparently was added by the twenty-third Tirthankara, which is the vow of celibacy—in the case of married people, after they have produced children.

The three jewels of Jainism are stated to be right belief, right knowledge and right conduct. Right belief is divided into eight subgroups. The first is that the believer must be free from doubt. The second is that there should be no expectation of reward. The third is that there should be no disgust at anything. The fourth is that no belief should be superstitious. The fifth states that no fault should be found. The sixth is complete steadiness of mind. The seventh is an affection for co-religionists. The eighth is the enhancement of the glory of the faith. Likewise, there are said to be five wrong beliefs. One is the belief in *ekanta,* which is that there can only be one point of view. The second is *viparita,* which is something which is perverse and contrary to reason and has to be condemned. The third is *samshaya,* where a person doubts or is a sceptic. The fourth is *vinaya,* veneration of good and bad equally, and the fifth is *agyan,* which is ignorance. Sufferings also are said to be of many kinds, which include hunger, thirst, cold, heat, insect bites, etc.

When it comes to the second jewel, that is right knowledge, it is again subdivided into eight parts. First and foremost, it is important to be literate, to be able to read and write. Secondly, it is important to understand what is read and what is written. The third is to understand generally apart from what is written. The fourth is to be punctual. The fifth is to have reverence for those who deserve reverence. The sixth is correct behaviour. The seventh is zeal in whatever is to be done. And the eighth is the sharing of knowledge.

Right conduct is nothing other than the five vows that we have already encountered, which are taken up by every Jain monk. Non-violence, which is the first of these vows, is the most important, and violence is also subdivided into what is intentional and what is non-intentional.

What is done, for example, by way of domestic chores or what is done in self-defence are said to be non-intentional and have different consequences.

Each Jain is given six daily duties. The first is to worship the saints of the religion. The second is to worship the guru or teacher. The third is to study scriptures. The fourth is to control the senses and the mind. The fifth is to lead an austere life, and the sixth is to do charity.

We are also told that if one wishes to become a Tirthankar in this life, then one has to inculcate sixteen qualities. The first is right belief of a slightly different kind—that is freedom from doubt, freedom from desire, freedom from revulsion and freedom from superstition. Do not proclaim the faith of others, cling to the truth, love another brother or sister on the path of liberation, and propagate the path of liberation once it is reached. The second is a reverence for the means of liberation. The third is to observe the five vows which all monks and lay people must observe. The fourth is ceaseless pursuit of knowledge. The fifth is apprehension of misery. The sixth is giving, in the widest sense, to others. The seventh is the practising of austerity. The eighth is to protect other mendicants or the path to nirvana. The ninth is to reward those who have spiritual merit. The tenth is devotion to *arhant*s or persons on the way to liberation. The eleventh is devotion to *acharya*s or teachers. The twelfth is devotion to a *upadhyay* or a saint who is a teacher. The thirteenth is the devotion to reading scriptures and practising them. The fourteenth is the six daily duties of every child. The fifteenth is the propagation of liberation. And the sixteenth is the affection to brothers on the path of liberation.

A very important part of Jain philosophy is the doctrine of *anekantavad* and *syadvad*. Anekantavad means that it is important to realize that there is always more than one point of view. Syadvad or *saptabhangi* is the use of seven different types of judgements which either affirm or negate. All knowledge therefore is said to be relative. Every proposition yields only a maybe or a *syad;* nothing can be affirmed or denied absolutely. The seven ways in which this doctrine works is that there is from each point of view of a substance or attribute that which is; that which is not; that which is and is not; that which is unpredictable; that which is and is not unpredictable; that which is not and is unpredictable; and that which is, is not and is unpredictable.

The first would mean that which is, that is from the point of view of its own material, place, time and nature. For example, a jar is a thing made of clay. A room is a particular shape and size. The second, *syad nasti,* is that a thing is not. The jar does not exist as made of metal, in a different place or time or in a different shape. The third which is *syad asty eva syan nasty eva* of relating to itself and another thing. It may be said that a thing is and a thing is not. In a certain sense the jar exists, in a certain sense it does not as it is only something which is made out of clay, which exists. The fourth, the *syad avaktavya,* is that a thing is unpredictable. Though the presence of its own nature and the absence of others are both in the jar, still, it becomes impossible to say what they really are. The fifth which is *syad asti avaktavya* is that from the point of view of itself and something else which is nothing, a thing is and is not predictable. The sixth which is *syad nasti avaktavya* a thing is not and is also unpredictable. Here again, a thing is not, and therefore, is indescribable. And the last *syad asti nast avaktavya* is that at the same time a thing is, is not and again is indescribable. We best bring out the indescribability of a thing by stating what it is and thereafter, what it is not. All judgements, therefore, are double-edged in their character.

The Jain path to liberation is extreme non-violence to every other sentient being while mortifying oneself. It can truly be stated to be an extremely ascetic and difficult religion to follow. As a matter of fact, in Jain theory, not only is one vegetarian but one cannot take the life of even a plant or a vegetable; therefore one should only survive on what is yielded up by the Earth. A morbid side of this faith is *sallekhana* or the gradual ebbing out of one's life at the end of one's life where one stops eating food, then drinking water until death finally arrives. Nirvana is said to be reached by this process, having led one's life in accordance with all the principles that have been laid down. And as we have seen, nirvana is essential to cross over to a world in which we leave behind reincarnation in the sense of a soul transmigrating from an amoeba to an animal or human life and life in heaven and hell. Incidentally, each jiva is supposed to take a different shape, depending on which body it is housed in, and only when it is finally released from the bondage of transmigration does it go back to its eternal and completely blissful state.

Buddhism

This religion revolves around the birth of one of the greatest teachers in history. He was born Siddharth or He Who Has Achieved His Aim. His family name was Gautam. His father was Suddhodana and his mother, Maya. He was the son of a king, heir to the Sakya kingdom, and was brought up in Kapilavastu, which was the capital of the Sakyas, by a foster mother, his own mother having died seven days after he was born. His birth was said to be miraculous. His mother got a dream that a white elephant had entered her as a result of which the Buddha was conceived, and it is said that he was born not in the usual way, but came out of the right side of his mother.

He married his cousin Yashodhara and had a son called Rahul, both of whom later became his disciples. As a prince, his father tried to shield him from the real world but he met an aged man bowed down by years, a sick man who had fever, a corpse which was being taken down the street with mourners who were weeping, and an ascetic priest who went past him, leaving an indelible impression on him that the world was a miserable place to live in. The result was that at the age of twenty-nine, he ran out of his home in the stealth of night, seeking the truth. He put on a yellow robe and went begging. He found five friends, and with them he went into the jungles of Uruvela. There, he almost died in an attempt to become an ascetic.

After six years of living an ascetic's life, he became convinced of the futility of this extreme method of attempting to discover the cause of all suffering. He then took to meditation and prayer, seated under a Bodhi tree. He resolved to himself that he would not stir until he attained supreme and absolute wisdom. After spending seven weeks under that tree, he finally attained Enlightenment and went about preaching to mankind about how to alleviate suffering, for the next forty years of his life. He visited his father's court twelve years after he had left it, and counted his father, his foster mother, wife and son among those who became his disciples, apart from his favourite disciple, Ananda, who was also his cousin. He died eating infected pork that was given by Chunda, a blacksmith who belonged to a low caste. He ate the pork knowing that it would lead to his death in order that Chunda not be offended. He gave orders that sweet rice and cakes must be given to all around him and what was left of the wild boar should be buried in a hole. After his death, his religion spread in the East and got divided into what is known as Mahayana, the Great Vehicle, or Hinayana or Theravada, which is the Sayings of the Elders, also called the Lesser Vehicle. It spread to Tibet, China, Japan and Korea and, after the eight century CE, lost ground in the country of its birth.

The moment the Buddha attained Enlightenment, the five ascetics who were with him came to hear what was the first sermon that was delivered by him. He told them of four noble truths. One, that there is suffering. Two, that such suffering has a cause which is desire beyond what is necessary. Three, that once such desire beyond what is necessary is extinguished, it will lead to the extinguishment of suffering. The fourth noble truth is the Eightfold Path through which one can obtain the cessation of such desire and therefore, suffering.

The first noble truth, the truth about suffering, was stated by the Buddha thus: birth is painful, decay is painful, disease is painful, death is painful, union with the unpleasant is painful. Painful is the separation from the pleasant, and any craving that is unsatisfied, that too is painful.

In brief, body, feeling, perception, will and consciousness, or the five *skanda*s, which spring from attachment, are all painful. In the *Samyutta Nikaya*, the Buddha stated:

> The *samsara* or life of all beings has its beginning in eternity. No opening can be discovered from which creatures who are mazed in ignorance and fettered by a thirst for being, stray and wander. What do you think disciples, what is more—the water in the four great oceans, or the tears that have been shed by you while you strayed and wandered in this *samsara*, and 'sorrowed' and wept because that was your portion? A mother's death, a brother's death, the loss of relatives, the loss of property— all this have you experienced through long ages. And while

you experience this, more tears have flown from you and
have been shed by you.

When it came to the cause of suffering, the Buddha told
these five ascetics: 'Now this is the noble truth of the origin
of suffering. Verily, it is the craving, thirst that causes the
renewal of becoming, that is accompanied by sensual delight
and seeks satisfaction now here, now there—that is to say,
the craving for gratification of the senses, or the craving
for prosperity.' The third noble truth then tells us how it
is possible to get out of this craving: by extinguishing such
craving. The fourth noble truth gives us the famous Eightfold Path to get out of such craving.

> There are two extremes which he who has gone forth ought
> not to follow—habitual devotion, on the one hand, to
> passions and pleasure of sexual/ sensual things and habitual
> devotion, on the other hand, to self-mortification, which is
> painful, ignoble and unprofitable. There is a middle Path
> discovered by me, a Path which opens the eyes and bestows
> understanding, which leads to peace, to insight, to higher
> wisdom and finally, to *Nirvana*. Verily, it is the Aryan Eight-
> fold Path, that is to say Right Beliefs, Right Aspirations,
> Right Speech, Right Conduct, Right Mode of Livelihood,
> Right Effort, Right Mindedness and Right Insight.

Right Belief is the first and most important on the Path
of Liberation. Right Belief or Right Views consist of

freedom from superstition and delusion, and dwelling on the Four Noble Truths that have been stated by the Buddha. Right Aim or Aspiration speaks of earnestness and nobility: right vision, a longing for renunciation. Right Speech must necessarily include an abstention from falsehood, backbiting, harsh language and frivolous talk. Right Action simply defined would mean unselfish action without indulging in rituals, prayer, spells and/ or sacrifice. When asked about ritual, the Buddha stated that anger, drunkenness, deception, envy—all associated with ritual spells and sacrifice—constitute uncleanliness, not the eating of flesh. And again, neither abstinence, nor going naked, nor shaving the head, nor a rough garment or offerings to priests or sacrifices to the gods will cleanse a man who is not free from delusion. Right Action obviously then leads to Right Living, that is abstention from lying, deceit, fraud.

Right Effort consists in controlling the passions. The Buddha recommended five methods by which to do this: First, to think of a good idea. Second, face the danger of the consequences of letting a bad idea develop into action. Third, move away from the bad idea. Fourth, analyse its antecedents and nullify all impulses to act in accordance therewith. Fifth, force the mind with the aid of the body to follow up the good idea. Right Effort would mean the practice of purity and the avoidance of mental unsteadiness. Insight or *pragna* and Right Meditation which is the result of being tranquil, would then lead one to *dhyan*, which is the highest contemplation and takes the place of prayer in

Buddhism. Dhyan itself has four stages. First, gladness and joy arising from a life of solitude accompanied by insight, reflection, contemplation and enquiry, which is free of all sensual pleasure. Second, internal calm and peace of mind. Third, absence of passion and prejudice where the mind becomes completely still and fourth, complete tranquillity, without care, and joy.

The Buddha emphasized ethics and logic, and shied away from metaphysics as something which one should avoid as being unnecessary to getting relief from suffering. He explained it beautifully in an allegorical story. He said a man had been shot with a poisoned arrow and refused treatment until he knew about who the person who shot him was, by what bow was he shot, by what arrow, and thus he died. The only relevant thing was not done by this man: that is, how he should recover from the poisoned arrow so that he could continue to live. This parable gives us the essence of Buddha's teaching: that it makes no difference to the immediate cause of suffering as to whether there is or isn't a God and as to whether the Universe existed, or was created. As a matter of fact, the Buddha tells us that the idea of a first cause does not, in any sense, help us to progress morally. If God exists, He must be the sole cause of all that happens— good as well as evil—and to conceive of evil coming from an all-good God is difficult. Equally, a person has no freedom of will if everything is predestined and created by God. If we expect to be forgiven by the grace of God then we can be tempted to live the life of a criminal and ultimately ask for

God's grace instead of leading a virtuous life and cultivating character.

Suffering then is intelligible only through the law of karma, which exists by itself and does not need a God to be its creator. There is no divine being who created us; man is born from his own deeds or his own karma. In a conversation with Anathapindika, a wealthy patron, the Buddha is said to have stated:

> If the world had been made by Ishwar, there should be no change nor destruction, there should be no such thing as sorrow or calamity, or right or wrong, seeing that all things pure and impure must come from Him. If sorrow and joy, love and hate, which spring up in all conscious beings be the work of Ishwar, He Himself must be capable of sorrow and joy, love and hatred—and if He has these, how can He be said to be perfect? If Ishwar be the Maker, and if all beings have to submit silently to their Maker's power, what would be the use of practising virtue? The doing of right or wrong would be the same, as all deeds are His making and must be the same with their Maker. But if sorrow and suffering are attributed to another cause, then there would be something of which Ishwar is not the cause. Why then should not all that exists be uncaused too? Again, if Ishwar be the Maker, He acts with or without purpose—if He acts with a purpose, He cannot be said to be all-perfect for a purpose necessarily implies satisfaction of a want. If He acts without a purpose, He must be like a lunatic

or a suckling babe. Besides if Ishwar be the Maker, why should not people reverently submit to Him? Why should they offer supplications to Him when sorely pressed by necessity? And why should people adore more Gods than one? Thus the idea of Ishwar is proved false by rational argument and all such contradictory assertions should be exposed.

He went on to state:

If by the Absolute, is meant something out of relation to all known things, its existence cannot be established by any reasoning. How can we know that anything unrelated to other things exists at all? The whole Universe as we know it is a system of relations. We know nothing that is or can be unrelated. How can that which depends on nothing or is related to nothing produce things which are related to one another and depend for their existence upon one another? Again, the Absolute is one or many. If it be only one, how can it be the cause of different things which originate, as we know, from different causes? If there be as many different Absolutes as there are things, how can the latter be related to one another? If the Absolute pervades all things and fills all space, then it also cannot also make them for there is nothing to make.

Further, if the Absolute is devoid of all qualities, all things arising from it ought likewise to be devoid of qualities. But in reality, all things in the world are circumscribed throughout by qualities. Hence the Absolute cannot be their cause. If the Absolute be considered to be different from qualities, how does it continually create the things possessing such qualities and manifest itself in them? Again, if the Absolute be unchangeable, all things should be unchangeable too. For the effect cannot differ in nature from the cause. But all things in the world undergo change and decay. How can the Absolute be unchangeable? Moreover, if the Absolute which pervades all is the cause of everything, why should we seek liberation? For we ourselves possess the Absolute and must patiently undergo every suffering and sorrow incessantly created by the Absolute.

Only perception and inference can lead to rational thought. Therefore, when the Buddha was asked questions as to whether God exists and as to whether the Universe always existed, he usually remained silent thereby indicating that whatever answer he gave would be utterly irrelevant to emancipating oneself from human suffering.

Another important doctrine that the Buddha taught was the Doctrine of Impermanence. His second lecture to the five ascetics spoke of this and said that there does not exist anything permanent such as a soul. He told them that the body is not an eternal soul for it tends towards destruction. Nor do feeling, perception, disposition and intelligence together constitute the eternal soul for were it so, it would not be the case that consciousness likewise tends towards destruction. Our form, feeling, perception, disposition and intelligence are all transitory and therefore, not permanent. That which is transitory and liable to change is not the eternal soul. So it must be said of all physical forms, past present or future, subjective or objective, far or near, high or low, this is not my eternal soul.

The Buddha preached that, as a matter of fact, a human being is a conglomerate of five skandas or the attributes just spoken of which, just as they came together at random, disperse at random on a person's death. The Buddha sometimes preached that Atman exists only in the sense of being the receiver of misery or happiness in successive lives as the reward of its own karma. But at most times, the Buddha taught that there is no Atman in the sense of a soul being created by God. He went on to state that there is no Self but there is only a transitory state of consciousness. There may be continuity but not identity. This he taught by the life of every human being. He said, 'You were once a baby, was that the same as you who are now grown up? The answer must be no. That child was something else, was one and I am another. It then follows that if a child, a grown up and an old person cannot be said to be the same person, then much less can it be said that after death the same person transmigrates and becomes a new person.' He also said that when a fire burns, you cannot possibly say that it is the same fire that is burning because every second the fire burning is a different fire, depending upon the fuel and other conditions such as the air that feeds it. He said that if one were able to identify oneself, it would come only from ignorance and not from the true knowledge of impermanence of all things.

He stated that the identity of objects is only another name for the continuity of becoming. Though the substance of our bodies as well as the constitution of our minds change from moment to moment, we still say that it is the same person. A thing is only a series of states, of which the first is said to be the cause of the second, for they seem to be of the same nature. The seeming identity from moment to moment consists in a continuity of moments which we may call the continuity of an ever-changing identity. All things undergo change in four stages: *utpada* (origin), *sthiti* (a particular state), *jara* (growth) and *nirodh* (destruction). Whatever exists from causes and conditions is impermanent and whatever has a cause must necessarily perish. This is the order of *kammaniyam* or cause and effect.

Another preaching spoke of *naam* and *roop,* naam being mental and roop being physical. The two, when connected together, spring into being together. The phenomena of the world are then divided into two roops—one, those having form, the four elements and their derivatives, which is roop, and *aroop*, that which does not have form. That is only phases of consciousness—the skandas or qualities of feeling, perception, synthesis and intellect. We are then told that it is *vigyan* which is the continuum of consciousness which transmigrates. Each unit of consciousness has three phases: *upada* (genesis), *thiti* (development) and *banga* (disillusionment). Each of these three exists and vanishes as soon as a moment of thought becomes past and is no longer present. There is, therefore, no absolute identity or absolute difference. The only continuity is the continuity of karma.

Another interesting doctrine that the Buddha taught is the doctrine of Dependent Origination. The Buddha put this doctrine thus:

> From ignorance springs the *samskaras*, from the *samskaras* springs consciousness, from consciousness spring name and form, from name and form spring the six senses, from the six senses spring contact, from contact springs sensation, from sensation springs thirst or desire, from desire springs attachment, from attachment springs becoming, from becoming springs birth, from birth springs old age and death, grief, lamentation, suffering, dejection and despair. Such is the origin of this whole mess of suffering. Again, in the destruction of ignorance, which consists in the complete destruction of lust, the *samskaras* are destroyed. By the destruction of the *samskaras*, consciousness is destroyed. By the destruction of consciousness, name and form are destroyed. By the destruction of name and form, the six senses are destroyed. By the destruction of the six senses, contact is destroyed. By the destruction of contact, sensation is destroyed. By the destruction of sensation, thirst is destroyed. By the destruction of thirst, attachment is destroyed. By the destruction of attachment, becoming is destroyed. By the destruction of becoming, birth is destroyed. By the

destruction of birth, old age and death, grief, lamentation, suffering, dejection and despair are destroyed. Such is the cessation of this whole mess of suffering..

Suffering is born from ignorance, or a false sense of 'I', or ego. The force of this ignorance is so great that in spite of the worst suffering, men display a great tenacity of clinging to life. The second link in the chain, samskaras, is a conglomerate of thirst. Thirst is the same as the thirst for desire or pleasure. Ultimately, the consciousness of 'I' does not reside in an eternal soul, but is a continuous phenomenon arising by way of cause and effect. Ignorance itself is not absolute; it comes into play so that it may abolish itself. When it comes to karma, each act is volitional—the first is the preparation for the act, the second is the act itself and the third is the backlash of the act or the feeling of regret or remorse. Every act has its retribution, either immediately or in the next existence. Acts are said to be those that are pure and those that are impure or tainted. A pure act, which is free from passion, desire and ignorance does not entail retribution and therefore prepares one for the way to nirvana. Meditation on the Four Noble Truths, by which one enters the path of getting to nirvana in this life itself, is a pure act, above good and evil. Good acts are those which lead to the conquest of passions, desires, illusions and the ego. Bad acts are those which are done to gain pleasure and have retributive consequences which lead to the bondage of birth and rebirth.

Insight, or prajna, and dhyan, or the highest contemplation, are the greatest tools on the path to nirvana. Dhyan itself has four stages. The first is gladness and joy arising from a life of solitude accompanied by insight, reflection, contemplation and inquiry, freed from all sensuality. Second, a sense of elation thanks to internal calm and peace of mind. Third, absence of all passions and prejudices; and fourth, complete tranquillity, after which a person is ready to attain nirvana. Ideal virtues which must accompany both insight and dhyan are charity, purity of conduct, patience, strenuous meditation, intelligence, employment of the right means, resoluteness, strength and knowledge. Self-control is very important in that it then avoids all evil such as murder, theft, adultery, lying, slander, abuse, idle talk, covetousness, hatred and error.

The Buddha spoke of heaven and hell, stating that on the dissolution of the body, the one who has done good is born in some happy state in heaven or conversely, in an unhappy state in hell. The Buddha did not like the caste system and redefined it: persons who are free from sin, free from haughtiness, having self-restraint, can be called brahmins. Persons who give way to anger and hatred, and are wicked, hypocritical, deceitful and embrace wrong views, are the ones who are the real outcastes.

Buddhism speaks of three jewels: the first is the Buddha, the second is Dharma or the Buddha's doctrine, and the third is the Sangha, which is a kind of Buddhistic brotherhood or religious order. The Sangha consists of both men and women who are monks as well as lay people. Initially, the Buddha was opposed to women entering the Sangha but later gave in after his cousin Ananda pointed out that half of humanity could not be excluded.

We now come to the difficult concept of nirvana in Buddhism. Nirvana can occur while a person is alive or on the person's death. The first is called *upadhisesha,* where human passions are extinct; in *anupadhisesha,* all being is extinct. Nirvana in Buddhism is said to be a state in which all suffering that is caused by desire is finally at an end. It is spoken of as being like the blowing out of a candle. The Buddha attained nirvana while he was still alive and it is in this sense that one can be alive even after having attained nirvana. On death, however, nirvana is a state in which one ceases to be, in the sense that nothing, not even one's consciousness, transmigrates. In this sense, Nirvana in Buddhism is really a complete cessation of being even though in the Nirvana Sutra, which a much later work, nirvana is described as bliss which is eternal and pure. It is difficult to reconcile to this positive view of nirvana when the Buddha's teachings expressly speak of cessation—that is cessation of all passion and desire when one is alive, and cessation of being at one's death.

The Buddha, in his famous 'Fire Sermon', spoke of persons who are burning with the fire of delusion and desire. This fire must be extinguished by being dispassionate, by being detached and following the Eightfold Path. On his death, the Buddha told his disciples to hold to the truth as the only lamp of illumination and each one to be a refuge to himself or herself. There is to be no external guide. It is only his teachings that one must comprehend by oneself so as to attain Nirvana.

Mahayana and Hinayana

After the Buddha died, the First Buddhist Council was convened around 483 BCE in which rules governing the Sangha were established, and the Buddha's true teachings were separated from the legends that had grown around him. However, it was at the Second Council, of 383 BCE, when different factions arose. One group known as the Sthaviravada school declared that in accordance with the Buddha's teachings, each person should seek his own Enlightenment and work out for himself how to become an arhant so as to escape the wheel of transmigration. On the other hand, the Mahasanghika or the Great Congregation school took the example of Buddha's life and how he led it after he attained nirvana, that is complete selflessness in doing service to others and therefore taking the responsibility of preaching the doctrine so that all could attain nirvana. This Mahasanghika school ultimately gave way to what is called the Mahayana school of Buddhism.

According to this school, an arhant is a spiritual ascetic who used the Buddha's vision as a guide towards spiritual development, instructing persons how to so develop. They believed that such persons take vows to be born in the worst of places so that they can help people overcome suffering.

Secondly, they believed that only the present exists at all times—past and future are illusions which distract and trouble the mind. Third, there is no time; there is only an eternal present; and fourth, Enlightenment brings with it many other powers including the ability to communicate without speech. Mahayana believes in ten practices which one should adopt in one's daily life in order to reach perfection. First, the act of giving generously. Second, to be a moral person who is self-disciplined and who has virtuous conduct. Third, to be patient and to be able to endure obstacles that come in the way. Fourth, to have effort and perseverance in whatever one does. Fifth, to be single-minded in one's concentration. Sixth, to be wise—that is to have compassion for other living beings. Seventh, the right way to accomplish anything. Eighth, determination in working towards a goal. Ninth, the acquisition of spiritual power; and tenth, knowledge both of the nature of life and of oneself.

The Hinayana school, the Lesser Vehicle, rejected the Mahayana sutras and maintained their belief that each one must work out his own salvation. The Buddha is an eternal transcendent being who continues to exist. Therefore, the Sakyamuni Buddha did not die of dysentery, but continues to be active in the lives of persons who exist. Hinayana uses various practices of meditation to transform body, speech and mind. The transformation of the body is through the practice of controlled bodily postures and gestures, which is called *mudra*. Second, transformation of speech is through the recitation of sacred psalms. Third, transformation of the mind is through the practice of concentration. These three practices then lead to a state of *samadhi* or stillness, finally leading to the cutting off of all sense perception and the emptying of the mind so that it is possible to shrug off this world of opposites with its karmic residues, and obtain nirvana.

Zen Buddhism

Zen Buddhism is a sect of Buddhism which has sprung from the Mahayana school, and is prevalent in China and Japan. Zen teachings can be likened to the finger pointing at the moon, which is an awakening, a realization of the unimpeded interpenetration of all things. Zen speaks of meditation as a most potent technique in which to experience bliss and is a better method than the reading of scriptures. Zen teachings tell us that insight is only the awakening of our mind which is in slumber. It is called 'subitism', which is that such experience comes suddenly at one shot, altogether, and not successively, one after another. In short, Enlightenment occurs in a single transformation that is total and instantaneous. Zen practices to awaken a person, therefore, can be anything that startle a person into Enlightenment. Maybe even a sudden jerk or a hitting on the head.

Confucianism

Confucius lived in the sixth century BCE. His father was much older than his mother. When he was three, his father died, and when he was seventeen, his mother died. He attracted many students during his lifetime because of his teachings. Though of noble birth, his poverty as a child must have led to a life of contemplation and noble thoughts. He loved music. He both sang and played the instruments that were available at the time. He was famous for saying that at fifteen he set his mind on study; at thirty, he felt that he had established himself; at forty, he had no doubts; at fifty, he knew what the choice of heaven was; at sixty, his ears got tuned to heaven; and at seventy, he followed his heart's desires, without going beyond the bounds of proper behaviour. He insisted on simple living and insisted that he did not possess wisdom. He was married, had a son and a daughter, and died at the ripe age of seventy-two.

He spoke of how one ought to try to become a 'superior man' as he was concerned only with how one should live life in the present. He was not concerned with the future. And like the Buddha, he wished to emphasize the importance of life, not the afterlife. According to him, a superior man is one who, first and foremost, believes in filial piety. Confucius advised one to follow their parents and not to disobey them. Serve them and then bury them with proper ritual, he said. And after they are dead, remember them as your ancestors. The maximum that one can do when they are alive is to remonstrate against them gently, if one does not agree with what they say, but ultimately do not act against their wishes, was his advice. The family is the single most important thing, and filial piety teaches us to put others' interests before ours: this was considered by Confucius to be the root of all virtues.

Honesty and sincerity are what make a superior man and above all, the word ren (humanity). You are to be loyal to the person who rules you, but you can criticize the ruler as well, so that he understands the difficulties of those who are governed. It is important to do what is right with knowledge. Therefore, learn history, poetry and learn how to perform rituals. And do this for its own sake.

Confucius' superior man is said to have as his only object, the truth. He was never tired of saying that the superior man thinks always of virtue, while the common man thinks of comfort. The superior man understands what is right whereas the inferior man understands what will sell. The superior man is modest in his speech but immodest in his actions. The superior man does not even act contrary to virtue. In moments of haste, he cleaves to it. In seasons of danger, he also cleaves to it. The superior man makes the difficulty to be overcome his first passion; success only comes later.

To Confucius, it is important to live life with courage, that is to see what is right and then go ahead and do it. Understanding of human nature, sympathy and compassion are important attributes of a superior man in dealing with his fellow men. He stressed the negative golden rule of not doing to others what one will not do to oneself. He also taught that ritual must be performed properly but must never be devoid of morals. He taught that any virtue taken to extreme is excessive and then cuts into other virtues. It is therefore important to live a life within the golden mean. The example he gave was that one can be honest and truthful and at the same time be impolite; one can be loyal to one's country, and at the same time such patriotism may be at the cost of truth.

Above all, he preached that there is no strict rule that must be followed in all situations. Every situation must be taken on its own merits. The example he gave is that the general rule that one shall not kill must necessarily be breached if, for example, a child is being abducted and there is no hope of the child coming back. The abductor has to be done away with. Confucius believed that one should lead a good life so that it's a long life, have children and accumulate wealth through correct means. Life has to be lived in accord with virtue. Worship of one's ancestors is a very important aspect of life. Confucius rejected magic and was a pacifist who believed strongly in non-violence. He also spoke badly of scholars who had studied the scriptures in order to search for their own salvation. To be a superior man is to follow virtue and be an example to others so that they are aided in obtaining salvation, according to Confucius.

Importantly, there is no God or afterlife in Confucianism. He was fond of telling people when asked about the afterlife, 'You do not understand life. How will you understand death?' When it came to government, he said that a government exists for the benefit of the people and can rule only if it has the mandate of heaven. Now, heaven in Confucianism is not a place but an ideal of what is a state of happiness. Confucianism does not look to the past or to the future, but only to this life and how to live it. He was fond of saying that the State must fill the subject's belly, not his mind; and strengthen his limbs, not his character. Too much knowledge, according to Confucius, is bad. Too much music, on the other hand, one can never have enough of as it promotes happiness.

Confucius spoke to us through his *Analects* which have come down to us, and his philosophy is best stated in his own words:

Life is really simple, but we insist on making it complicated.

It does not matter how slowly you go as long as you do not stop. I hear and I forget. I see and I remember. I do and I understand. Everything has beauty, but not everyone sees it.

Our greatest glory is not in never falling, but in rising every time we fall. Real knowledge is to know the extent of one's ignorance.

To know what you know and what you do not know, that is true knowledge.

By three methods we may learn wisdom: First, by reflection, which is noblest; Second, by imitation, which is easiest; and third by experience, which is the bitterest.

When anger rises, think of the consequences.

It is easy to hate and it is difficult to love. This is how the whole scheme of things works. All good things are difficult to achieve; and bad things are very easy to get.

Success depends upon previous preparation, and without such preparation there is sure to be failure.

Better a diamond with a flaw than a pebble without.

If you think in terms of a year, plant a seed; if in terms of ten years, plant trees; if in terms of 100 years, teach the people.

He who learns but does not think, is lost! He who thinks but does not learn is in great danger.

Humility is the solid foundation of all virtues. Only the wisest and stupidest of men never change.

The strength of a nation derives from the integrity of the home. To be wronged is nothing unless you continue to remember it. Study the past, if you would divine the future.

We should feel sorrow, but not sink under its oppression. You cannot open a book without learning something.

In a country well governed, poverty is something to
be ashamed of. In a country badly governed, wealth is
something to be ashamed of.

Learning without thought is labour lost; thought
without learning is perilous. An oppressive government
is more to be feared than a tiger.

Death and life have their determined appointments;
riches and honours depend upon heaven.

To practise five things under all circumstances
constitutes perfect virtue; these five are gravity, generosity
of soul, sincerity, earnestness, and kindness.

Wisdom, compassion, and courage are the three
universally recognized moral qualities of men.

Virtue is never left to stand alone. He who has it will
have neighbours.

He who speaks without modesty will find it difficult
to make his words good.

After Confucius died, he had two important followers who
expounded on his doctrine. One was Mencius, who was born
in the fourth century BCE. According to Mencius, human
nature is essentially good and consists of compassion, that
is, humanity. Doing what is right is important. Reverence
for one's ancestors is also important, which leads to ritual.
Second is a sense of shame. The third is a sense of modesty.
And the fourth is a sense of what is right and what is wrong.
Only human beings reflect what is the goodness of heaven,
as human beings are essentially moral entities.

Mencius was followed by Xinxi, who was of the opinion that Mencius was not correct. Human nature according to Xinxi is evil. Being selfish and simply following one's nature will lead to selfish and, therefore, evil acts. Rightness is born from artificiality, that is from the mind telling the human being that what his nature is must be changed. Heaven was described by Xinxi as being nothing other than nature which knows no morality. He gave as an example the sun which shines on the good and the evil alike.

Confucianism has been explained in several books, four of them being of importance: the *Analects*, of Confucius, *The Sayings of Mencius*, *The Great Learning* and the *Doctrine of the Mean*.

Taoism

The great philosopher and thinker Lao Tzu lived in the sixth century BCE in China and was a contemporary of Confucius. The Tao Te Ching, which is a collection of his sayings, is a fundamental book that explains this abstruse and mysterious religion. In Lao Tzu's own words, the following description of Tao shows us how difficult it is as a concept:

> There was something undifferentiated and yet complete, which existed before Heaven and Earth. Soundless and formless it depends on nothing and does not change. It operates everywhere and it is free from danger. It may be considered the mother of the universe. I do not know its name, I call it Tao.

Tao has been described as being silent, obscure and indistinct. It is a mysterious un-nameable being which is the source of all existence, being prior to the Universe itself. Tao also believes that each human being is a microcosm of the cosmos and therefore, can find the Tao within himself.

An important concept in Tao is Ziran. It is usually a spontaneous thing which is set to flow by itself along with the Tao. It is like the Universe which exists by itself and is sufficient unto itself. If you are to flow with nature, you free yourself of selfishness and desire, and live simply. Another concept is called the De which results from living and cultivating the Tao, which can be done only by practising ethics. *Wei Wu Wei* is said to be 'action without action' which is to be within the flow of things, never resisting them. It involves the letting go of the ego, which is an extremely difficult thing. The Tao Te Ching says if you act actively, you will ruin things. The sage acts with inaction.

In Wei, a person seeks to come into harmony with Tao himself, which is accomplished by non-action. Tao consists of three treasures stated to be *jing*, that is one's very essence; *qi*, which is the material force of the Universe, and *shen*, which is the consciousness of the spirit.

It is by practising these three things in accordance with Taoist philosophy that one achieves complete serenity in life. Like Confucianism, the Tao concentrates on this life and does not have reference to any developed after life. Also, the Tao is to be distinguished from a Creator God which does not exist in Taoism. Coming back to Taoist ethics, what is stressed is naturalness, spontaneity, simplicity and detachment from desire. Three treasures of Taoism are stated to be compassion, moderation and humility, which translate themselves into an abstention from war and simplicity of living in accordance with nature.

Another interesting concept is the concept of Yin and Yang. Tao explains that Tao in the beginning rested in deep chaos. It then evolved into a cosmic unity full of creative potential. This unity then brought forth two energies, Yin and Yang, which in turn merged in harmony to create a combination from which all life came forth. Yin and Yang are opposite principles which bring forth life as strong and weak, light and dark, soft and hard, etc. Taoism believes in gods who exist in another world, that is in a celestial world—spirits who hover around the Earth and persons who live in the netherworld. The Xian are those human beings who have achieved a life of living in harmony with Tao.

Practices or virtues are taught in a book called the *Scriptural Statutes of Lord Lao*. These practices are as follows:

1. Non-action,
2. Softness and weakness
3. Guarding all things feminine
4. Being nameless.
5. Being still
6. Being adept at what one does
7. Having no desire
8. Contentment
9. To know how to yield and withdraw

Taoism teaches that one must avoid killing of both human beings and animals, theft, sexual misconduct, lying, and the use of intoxicants. It also teaches one how to look after one's own family and one's own kith and kin; how to support a person who does good; how to support a person who is unfortunate and to make him recover or get back to his former state; how never to have thoughts of revenge even if somebody does harm to one; and the expectation that one will attain the Tao only as long as all beings attain the Tao.

Many meditation techniques of Taoism are various practices which are magical in nature, and which attempt to explain the spirit world and cultivate longevity in life. This obscure and difficult faith is perhaps best explained in some of the sayings of its founder, Lao Tzu. Some of them are:

To the mind that is still, the whole universe surrenders.

Life is a series of natural and spontaneous changes. Don't resist them—that only creates sorrow. Let reality be reality. Let things flow naturally forward in whatever way they like.

Do the difficult things while they are easy and do the great things while they are small.

The journey of a thousand miles must begin with a single step. Mastering others is strength. Mastering yourself is true power. He who knows, does not speak. He who speaks, does not know. Silence is a source of great strength.

Knowing others is wisdom, knowing yourself is Enlightenment. A good traveller has no fixed plans, and is not intent on arriving.

Nothing is softer or more flexible than water, yet nothing can resist it.

Life and death are one thread, the same line viewed from different sides.

By letting it go it all gets done. The world is won by those who let it go. But when you try and try, the world is beyond the winning.

Health is the greatest possession. Contentment is the greatest treasure. Confidence is the greatest friend. Non-being is the greatest joy.

Treat those who are good with goodness, and also treat those who are not good with goodness. Thus goodness is attained. Be honest to those who are honest, and be also honest to those who are not honest. Thus honesty is attained.

Manifest plainness, embrace simplicity, reduce selfishness, have few desires.

The wise man does not lay up his own treasures. The more he gives to others, the more he has for his own.

The softest things in the world overcome the hardest things in the world.

If you realise that all things change, there is nothing you will try to hold on to. If you are not afraid of dying there is nothing you cannot achieve.

The sage does not hoard. The more he helps others, the more he benefits himself. The more he gives to others, the more he gets himself. The Way of Heaven does one good but never does one harm. The Way of the sage is to act but not to compete.

Violence even when well intentioned, always rebounds upon oneself.

Without stirring abroad, one can know the whole world; without looking out of the window one can see the way of heaven. The further one goes, the less one knows.

All things in the world come from being. And being comes from non-being.

Heaven is long-enduring, and earth continues long. The reason why heaven and earth are able to endure and continue this long is because they do not live of, or for, themselves.

All difficult things have their origin in that which is easy, and great things in that which is small.

To realise that you do not understand is a virtue; not to realise that you do not understand is a defect.

The higher the sun ariseth, the less shadow doth he cast; even so the greater is the goodness, the less doth it covet praise; yet cannot avoid its rewards in honours.

He who knows others is wise. He who knows himself is enlightened. How could man rejoice in victory and delight in the slaughter of men?

The Tao that can be told is not the eternal Tao; the name that can be named is not the eternal name. The Nameless is the origin of Heaven and Earth; the Named is the mother of all things.

Man takes his law from the Earth; the Earth takes its law from Heaven; Heaven takes its law from the Tao. The law of the Tao is its being what it is.

It is better to do one's own duty, however defective it may be, than to follow the duty of another, however well one may perform it. He who does his duty as his own nature reveals it, never sins.

Part III: Hinduism

The Vedas

The oldest spoken hymns that have come down to mankind are compiled together in what is known as the Rigveda. 'Veda' essentially means knowledge and 'Rig' means praise, so the entire compilation is really a title which praises knowledge. This compilation is said to date back to sometime in 2000 BCE and spanned at least 1000 years. It is made up of ten mandalas or books which consist of 1028 hymns, which in turn have 10,552 mantras.

There are some 414 rishi families that are associated with the hymns of the Rigveda. The most prominent among them being the Angiras family responsible for 3619 mantras, the Kanwa family for 1315 mantras, the Vashishta family for 1276 mantras, Visvamitra for 983 mantras, Athri for 885 mantras, Brighu and his family for 473 mantras, Kashyapa for 415 mantras, Grihatsamada for 401 mantras, the great sage Agastya for 316 mantras, and Bharat and his family for 170 mantras. Mandalas 1 and 10 were written last, both consisting of 191 hymns each.

The gods and goddesses of the Rigveda are largely nature divinities such as fire, water, the sky, the sun, etc. The maximum number of hymns are sung to Agni, who is the

God of Fire, and Indra. Indra is referred to as the king of the gods and as a great *soma* drinker (soma being an intoxicating substance which itself is deified, a full mandala, no. 9, being devoted to it). Soma lures Agni away from the waters and demons. Indra's family life is troubled. His birth is itself unnatural inasmuch as his mother, Aditi, kept him in her womb for many years in order to protect him, presumably because his father, Tvashtr (the artisan of the gods), was jealous of Indra's great powers. Indra ultimately kills his father. His greatest heroic deed is the killing of Vrittra or drought, as he is associated with the thunderbolt and, therefore, rain. He vanquishes drought so that rain can pour all over the Earth and give birth to vegetation.

We encounter many other interesting gods and goddesses. Dyauspitr is the Sky God who is the father of the gods (*pitr*, meaning father), and is equivalent to Zeus in the Greek pantheon of gods and Jupiter in the Roman pantheon. We also have Savitar to whom the famous Gayatri Mantra is sung (perhaps the most revered hymn of the Rigveda to Hindus today). Savitar is the rising and setting sun and is said to be the father of Surya, who is otherwise the Sun God. Mitra and Varun are important protectors of *rita* or cosmic order or righteousness and truth in man. They are both described as *asura*s or great lords, Mitra being associated with the fire ordeal and Varun with the water ordeal, as human beings took oaths in their name and called upon each of these gods to save them from either burning to death or drowning to death, respectively. We also have Pushan, the charioteer of the gods.

Rudra is another important deity. Though there are only three entire hymns in the Rigveda addressed to him, the ambivalence of his character points to an important development of Indian theology that culminates in the Hindu God Shiva. Rudra is fierce and destructive like a terrible beast or a wild storm. The Rigvedic seers beg him to turn his malevolence elsewhere. Yet, Rudra is not merely demonic for he is also a healer apart from his being the bringer of disease and destruction. Vishnu, an important God in the Hindu pantheon, is hardly invoked. There is an interesting hymn in which Vishnu's three strides encompass the Earth, the heavens and the nether world. Usha is another deity associated with the dawn, and Vayu, a deity associated with the wind. Rudra's children are said to be the Maruts, who are twin solar deities.

At this juncture, it is important to go to the creation hymns of the Rigveda. We will see, as we go through them, that they are interestingly speculative in nature and ultimately seem to veer towards One God. In mandala 10, hymn 72, Brahmanaspati (or the priest among the gods) is likened to a smith, who, by blasting and smelting, created existence from non-existence. Regions are then born from which spring the productive power, which in turn produces the Earth. Interestingly, Daksha is said to be born of Aditi and vice-versa. Daksha apparently is the male creative principle, as Aditi is the female creative principle. Aditi is also described as Daksha's daughter. Surya, the sun, is then spoken of, who was brought forward by the gods when he was lying hidden in the sea. Eight are the sons of Aditi, seven of whom are immortals and who are regarded as solar deities: Mitra, Varun, Dhata, Aryaman, Bhaga, Vivasvat and Surya. Both Mitra and Varun we have already come across as being protectors of *rita* or cosmic order or righteousness in man. Dhata is said to arrange things perfectly, giving order to Creation. Aryaman, which literally means companion, is the God of hospitality. Bhaga is the one who apportions wealth. Vivasvat is another solar deity who is said to be the father of Yama, who was the first person to have gone over to the planes of existence after dying on Earth, and is consequently regarded as the God of Death. Surya, who we have already come across, is the sun. Apart from these seven, Aditi gave birth to Martanda which literally translated means 'dead egg', and it is from this dead egg that mankind sprang forth. Martanda is the only child of Aditi not to be immortal but to have to suffer the pangs of death.

Another interesting Creation hymn speaks of Vishvakarma—mandala 10, hymns 81 and 82. Vishvakarma is referred to as the architect of the Universe who produced Earth and heaven, welding them with his arms. Interestingly, he is referred to as the primeval germ which the waters received. The gods were gathered together and rested upon the unborn's navel, that one wherein abide all things existing—an interesting first reference to an unborn Creator.

We then come to mandala 10, Verse 90, which is famously known as the Purushasukta. Purusha is a cosmic man, described as having a thousand heads, thousand eyes and thousand feet. He is the lord of immortality who waxes and becomes greater by ingesting food. All creatures are one-fourth of him, three-fourths being eternal in heaven. When the gods prepared the sacrifice with Purusha as their offering, its oil was spring, the gift was autumn, and summer was the wood. From that great sacrifice, the Samaveda hymns were born. The Yajur Veda was also born from Purush. When they divided Purusha, the Brahman was its mouth, from both his arms was the Kshatriya made, his thighs became the Vaishya and from his feet the Shudra was produced. The moon came from his mind and from his eye the sun had been born. Indra and Agni were born from his mouth, and Vayu from his breath. This hymn is the earliest reference to the *varna*s that make up Hindu society even today—the Brahman being the priest, the Kshatriya being the warrior, the Vaishya being the trader, and the Shudra being the person who serves the other three varnas.

Yet another creation hymn, mandala 10, hymn 121, speaks of *hiranyagarbha* or the golden egg. This golden cosmic egg became, by its grandeur, the sole ruler of the moving world that breathes and slumbers. By it, the heavens are strong and the Earth steadfast. The hymn ends stating that the God that is to be adored with oblations is Prajapati, the lord of all the creatures, having created all of them. Prajapati alone comprehends all created beings.

We now come to hymn 129, which is arguably the most important hymn relating to Creation in the entire Vedas. It begins by stating that at a particular point in time, there was neither existence nor non-existence. At that point, that one thing breathed by its own nature; apart from it, there was nothing whatsoever. Darkness there was and the void was filled by the great power of warmth which came because of desire in this being. The hymn goes on to ask 'Who verily knows and who can here declare it as to whence this being was born and whence comes creation? The Gods are later than the world's production, who knows then whence the world first came into being?' It then ends, stating, 'He, the first origin of this creation, whether he formed it at all or did not form it, whose eye controls this world in highest heaven, he verily knows it, or perhaps he knows not.'

The reference to one self-existent God also arises in mandala 1, hymn 164. In Verse 46, this hymn specifically states: 'They call him Indra, Mitra, Varuna, Agni, and he is heavenly nobly-winged Garutman, to what is One, sages give many a title they call it Agni, Yama, Matarisvan.' This verse is a very late verse of the Rigveda and seems to point directly to one God being named by the various deities of the Rigveda.

The famous Gayatri Mantra, which we have referred to earlier, occurs in mandala 3, hymn 62. In Verses 10–12, the mantra states:

May we attain that excellent glory of Savitar the God,
May he stimulate our prayers.

With understanding, earnestly, of Savitar the God
we crave Our portion of prosperity.

Men, singers, worship Savitar the God with hymns
and holy rites, Urged by the impulse of their thoughts.

What we see in the Rigveda is a positive attitude to life, an
attitude in which the making of wealth and the seeking of
pleasure, be it through drink or other ways, are extolled
and not frowned upon. There is no reincarnation in these
hymns but an onward progress to a heaven which is policed
by Yama and filled with song.

The other Vedas composed after the Rigveda are the
Samaveda and the Yajuraveda. The Samaveda consists of
six *adhyayas* or books in which there are 1875 mantras. As
many as 1800 mantras are from the Rigveda directly. This
Veda seems to have been composed between 1200 and 1000
BCE and is nothing but portions of the Rigveda which is
sung by Brahmin priests. The Yajuraveda, also belonging
roughly to this period, is divided into two parts, black and
white. Black denotes haphazard arrangement, whereas white
denotes an arrangement which is well thought out. This
Veda has forty *adhyayas*, or chapters, and 1975 mantras.
Out of which 1875 mantras are borrowed from the Rigveda
and built upon by various seers.

Each Veda is divided into four parts: the Samhita or hymn
section, the Brahmana or the ritual section, the Aryanaka or
forest treatises, and finally the Vedanta, or the end of the
Veda, which consists of pure philosophy, also called the

Upanishads. The Rigveda has attached to it the Aitareya and the Kaushitaki Upanishads, just as the Samaveda has attached to it the Chandogya and the Kena Upanishads. The Yajuraveda has attached to it the Brihadaranyaka, Isha, Katha, Taittiriya, Shvetashvatara and Maitrayaniya Upanishads. Also attached to it is a famous text called the Shatapatha Brahmana, which is the treatise of a hundred paths, which deals with rituals including the Ashvamedha sacrifice or the horse sacrifice performed by victorious kings, and the death rituals.

At the time of the Buddha, only three Vedas were referred to. A fourth Veda sprung into being thereafter, called the Atharvaveda. This Veda comprises twenty books, 730 hymns and 6000 mantras. It consists largely of dealing with evil spirits and diseases caused by them for which there are herbs, prayers and spells. Heaven is spoken of in book 4, hymn 34, and also consists of sexual pleasures. The Mundaka, Mandukya and Prashna Upanishads are appended to this Veda. Since the Sama, Yajura and Atharva Vedas are treatises which are not directly concerned with philosophical speculation, we can now proceed directly to the Upanishads in the order mentioned, beginning with the Rigveda's two Upanishads.

The Upanishads

There are 108 'Upanishads', which literally means a student sitting next to a guru to receive spiritual knowledge. The Upanishads selected for study in this chapter are the thirteen most important ones, which give an insight into Hindu philosophy. The great German philosopher Arthur Schopenhauer described them as 'the fruit of the highest human knowledge and wisdom, the kernel of which has at last reached us in the Upanishads as the greatest gift of this century'.

Aitareya Upanishad

This Upanishad consists of three chapters, the first of which speaks of *atman,* or an individual's soul. This atman is said to have existed all by itself prior to the creation of the Universe. It is this atman which is the creator of everything from itself. Creation came in stages: first came space, then the Earth and the stars, then light and the waters. After this came the cosmic man or the self, and sensations such as hearing, sight, reproductivity, etc. And then came the interdependence of living organisms, after which came man, who cogitated on himself, realizing he was more than just the sensory organs, the mind and the reproductive ability. To the question 'Who am I?', the answer was that I am the highest manifestation of atman, who is also known as *brahman*.

In the second chapter, this Upanishad states that procreation and the nurturing of children makes a man immortal, and that rebirth or transmigration is the means by which the same atman continues to exist in different forms in the Universe. It is also stated that the atman in human life is born thrice: first as a child; second, when the child reaches parenthood; and third, after death, when the atman transmigrates. The third chapter states that consciousness is above all, and that the key to the riddle of the Universe is one's own inner self. To know the Universe, know thyself. Importantly, the stress is on knowledge. Everything is produced by knowledge, rests on knowledge and is led by knowledge. Knowledge is the cause. Knowledge is brahman.

Kaushitaki Upanishad

In the first chapter of the Kaushitaki Upanishad, rebirth and transmigration of atman, the self, is produced by karma or the effects of one's deeds. Then follows a famous question: 'Is there liberation and freedom from these cycles?' The second chapter goes on to state that liberation comes only with the realization that a being's individual soul is identical with brahman or the universal spirit. In order to realize this, one does not need to pray. It goes on to state that external rituals must be replaced by the inner ritual of introspection. Not rituals but knowledge should be one's pursuit to reach this goal.

The third chapter invokes the deity Indra, personifies him as atman, and reveals that he is the life-breath, and atman is the conscious self. Obviously, speech cannot define a human being as people are born dumb. Likewise, neither can sight or hearing, as people are born blind and deaf. Also the mind cannot be said to define a human being as there are so many among us without the power of clear thinking. Ultimately, one can only know the self through one's own consciousness. This beautiful Upanishad goes on to say that life force and knowledge of the self alone bring bliss, the absence of ageing, and immortality. The last chapter of this Upanishad states that brahman and atman are one, and that there is ultimate unity in the self.

Chandogya Upanishad

The Chandogya Upanishad opens with a recommendation that a person should meditate on Om. It calls Om a song or a chant. It says that it was used in a struggle between the *deva*s or the gods and the *asura*s or the demons, both being races born from one creator, Prajapati. The Upanishad then goes on to state that every time Om was chanted by the gods, the demons cursed it and as a result, smell, speech, sight, hearing and the mind were all affected, having both good and evil in them. It is only when the gods chanted Om as *prana* or vital breath and the demons cursed it, that they were utterly destroyed. As a result of this, prana alone is free from evil and is inherently good. Om is the symbol of this life principle in man. The Upanishad then goes on to describe a debate between three men proficient in the chanting of Om, and the debaters then summarizing their discussion stating that the origin of this world is space, as everything arises and disappears back into space. Next, the Upanishad speaks of how ridiculous it is that priests go about reciting verses and singing hymns without the slightest idea as to what they are singing.

The second chapter of this Upanishad states that a chant is good for three reasons: because of goodness itself, friendship of people who chant together and wealth that arises therefrom. It then says that everything in the Universe is the chant of Om. In the same chapter, the Upanishad speaks of the three branches of dharma or religious life or duty: sacrifice, study by oneself and charity are the first branch; austerity is the second; and dwelling in the house of a guru for education is the third. The third chapter begins by talking about what is called Madhuvidya, or knowledge that is likened to honey. The sun is praised as the source of light and life and is worthy of meditation and is therefore described as the honey of all the Vedas. The rising and setting of the sun is likened to man's cycles of clarity and confusion, whilst knowing oneself and being one with the sun is a state of perfect knowledge or endless light, which knows no night. The Gayatri Mantra, which is the symbol of brahman or the universal spirit, must be sung as it protects everybody by its chant. We are then told that the light that shines above the highest heaven is higher than everything, beyond which there is nothing else, and that is the same light which is within oneself. Realise oneself, therefore. Life is then described as a celebration whose *dakshina,* or gift, is moral conduct which includes austerity, charity, non-hypocrisy, non-violence, telling the truth and gifts made to others.

The fourth chapter opens with the story of King Janasruti and a poor man, Raikva, who has only a cart. King Janasruti is pious, charitable, builds rest houses and does good deeds but lacks knowledge of the fact that one's atman is nothing but a reflection of the world spirit, the brahman. Raikva, on other hand, is poor and has sores on his skin, but he has knowledge of brahman. The Upanishad refers to the generous and rich king as a Shudra and the poor working man with the cart as a Brahman, that is one who knows brahman. In short, the story declares knowledge as superior to wealth and power, and also states that knowledge may be with the poorest person, while the seeker of knowledge may be someone wealthy and powerful.

Another interesting story is that of Satyakam who goes to a sage named Haridrumata Gautama and requests the sage's permission to study with him. When the sage asks him as to which family he comes from, he replies truthfully stating he does not know who his father is. The sage declares that the boy's honesty is the mark of a true Brahman, that is the true seeker of the knowledge of brahman, and accepts him in his school. Satyakam is sent to tend 400 cows and can return only when they multiply into 1000. He learns from the cows that the source of everything is brahman. When Satyakam grows up, he himself becomes a guru and teaches a boy called Upakosala. This boy has been studying for twelve years with his guru and learns that the path to brahman is not through penance but only through knowledge of the self.

In the fifth chapter of this Upanishad, it is stated that when a man knows the best, he becomes the best; when he knows excellence, he becomes excellent; when he knows success, he becomes successful. It goes on to speak of the doctrine of two paths and five fires in the afterlife. The two paths are stated to be Devayana, which is the path of the gods, and the Pitrayana, the path of the fathers. The path of the fathers in the afterlife is for those who live a life of rituals. They enter heaven but stay there in proportion to the good they have done, and then return to be reborn on Earth, depending on their past karma. The path of the devas is for those who live a life acquiring knowledge of brahman. These do not ever return and in their afterlife, merge with brahman. All existence is then said to be cycles of fire, the five fires being: the Universe, the clouds, Earth, man, woman and finally a baby, who when born is born from the fifth fire and returned to this fire on death. Interestingly, the Upanishad states that for the insect world, there is neither Devayana nor Pitrayana after death. It asserts that rebirth is the reason why the other world is never full, as living creatures live after death in the other world only temporarily while waiting to be reborn. The last part of the fifth chapter deals with five persons who seek the knowledge of Atman Vaishnavara, which means that the self is the same in all living beings. This knowledge was only with a particular king, Ashvapati Kaikeya. When the five persons are taught this, they realize the unity that is within all living beings, good or bad.

The sixth chapter contains the single most famous statement made in the Chandogya Upanishad, namely '*Tat tvam asi*' meaning 'That thou art'. It comes about as a result of a conversation between a father and a son, the father being Uddalaka Aruni and the son being Shvetaketu Arunaiya. The son is sent to school for twelve years and the father asks him whether he has learnt of that which cannot be perceived and cannot be known. The son correctly states that he hasn't learnt any such thing. Uddalaka then goes on to state that a Universe cannot be born from nothingness but is born from truth or reality, and is without a second from the very beginning. This truth gives birth to living beings through an egg, through a womb or from seeds. What is important is to realize that this eternal truth is the core of each living being and is therefore the core of the teaching leading to the famous expression, 'That thou art' (VI.9.4). The sixth chapter goes on to state that the self is like salt which is dissolved in water. It is everywhere in the water, cannot be seen, and yet exists. This self has always existed and will always exist, though it is imperceptible.

The seventh chapter opens with a conversation between Sanatkumar and Narada, the sage. Narada tells Sanatkumar that he knows all the Vedas, epics, history, rituals, politics, etc., but that none of these have led him to knowledge of the self. Sanatkumar then gives him what is called the knowledge which is progressive, a step-wise journey to attaining the self. He begins by stating that worldly knowledge is at the bottom of the ladder, above which is speech. Above speech is the mind and above mind, is will. Higher than will is *chitta* or consciousness and higher than consciousness is *dhyana* or contemplation. One must therefore revere contemplation as the manifestation of brahman. It is only then that *vigyana* or wisdom comes. Another progressive method is also outlined in stating that strength is good but then higher than strength is food because to be strong, one needs to be well nourished. Greater than food is water because without water one cannot grow food. Better than water is heat because it is heat, combined with the wind, that brings rain. And higher than heat is space because it is in space that the sun, moon and the stars bearing heat all reside. It then goes on to state that greater than space is memory and greater than memory is hope, hope that one might attain brahman. Greater than hope is prana, or the life breath. Ultimately he who knows the life breath becomes an *ativadi,* that is a speaker who has the confidence of a man who knows the self.

The eighth chapter of the Chandogya Upanishad speaks of the self as being one that is eternally free of grief, suffering or death; it is happy for all time. This is the real self. The false self is the material body, the dream state and the deep-sleep state. It is only what is beyond deep sleep that is true bliss, in which state a person is actually one with the entire Universe. This Upanishad, therefore, speaks of merger of atman with brahman as being the ultimate object which every human being can strive for.

Kena Upanishad

This Upanishad begins by asking as to what is the cause that sends out the mind, the first breath, the speech by which we speak, and then asks as to who is the deity or God that gives us eyes and ears so that we may see and speak. It then asserts that knowledge is outward and inward. What is outward is sensory, and what is inward is conceptual. Brahman is an abstract concept and we are told that there the eye goes not, speech goes not, nor the mind. It is other than the known and above the unknown. It is only our forebears that have told us this. Importantly, the Upanishad asserts that brahman cannot be worshipped because it is unthinkable and eternal. It is the inner essence of everything. It is what hears in the ears, what sees in the eyes, what smells in the breath and what comprehends meaning in thought.

The second chapter states that *moksha*, or self-realization, can only happen when the atman within one awakes. When that happens, such a person finds immortality and when he departs from this world, he becomes immortal. In the third chapter, the Upanishad then goes on to select three famous gods from the Rigveda and begins by telling us that in a war between the devas and the asuras, that is the gods and the demons, Brahman won a victory for the gods. The gods, however, praise themselves for the victory and not brahman. When brahman revealed itself before the gods, they did not recognize it. They looked upon it and said, 'What is this fantastic being?', and delegated Agni, the God of Fire, to discover who this being was. Agni rushed to brahman and boasted that he is able to burn whatever there is on earth. Brahman laid a piece of grass before Agni and said, 'Burn this.' Agni did his best to burn it and failed. He then returned to the gods and confessed, 'I am unable to discover who this wonderful being is.' The same then happened with Vayu, and Vayu, when confronted by brahman, said I am *matarisvan,* which is that which fills the space around Mother Earth and moves in space. Vayu boasted and said, 'I am able to carry and pull whatever there is on Earth.' Brahman placed a blade of grass before him and said, 'Carry this, then.' He too failed and returned to the gods and said, 'I am unable to discover who this wonderful being is.' The gods then turned to their King Indra, who is the God of Thunder and lightning. And when Indra went to brahman, the latter transformed into a beautiful woman called Uma. Indra asked Uma, 'Who are you?' Uma replied 'I am brahman, the one who obtained victory for you, O God, though you praise yourselves for it.' And it is at that point that Indra discovered brahman. And this is why Agni, Vayu and Indra are elevated above the other gods because these three met and experienced brahman first. This chapter makes it clear that brahman has to be experienced, and that cannot happen unless the ego is completely annihilated.

In the fourth chapter, the Upanishad ends by asserting that ethics is the foundation of the path to atman/ brahman. It says that penance and charity work are the foundation, the Vedas are the limb, and truth is the very backbone of brahman.

Brihadaranyaka Upanishad

The Brihadaranyaka Upanishad is the longest and the most exalted Upanishad and is known for its great statement: 'From untruth lead us to truth, from darkness lead us to light, from death lead us to immortality. Om! Peace, peace, peace.' It consists of three *kandas* or sections: the Madhu Kanda, which teaches the identity of the individual and universal self; the Muni Kanda, which is the philosophical justification of this teaching; and the Khila Kanda, which speaks of modes of worship and meditation. This Upanishad speaks of Prajapati, the lord of the creatures, who appears in the Rigveda and who creates the world, giving birth to devas as well as asuras. It eulogises the chant (the Samaveda) and breath, which upholds this world. It also has an Adam-and-Eve verse in which it goes on to state that in the beginning, the world was only the self, shaped like a man. He looked around and saw nothing but himself saying, 'I am'. He wanted to have a companion, so he split his body into two, one half becoming his female mate with whom he copulated to create human beings. The female then became a cow, the male being a bull, and produced cows. Likewise, the whole of animal creation took place in pairs, producing their young. It goes on to describe the true nature of atman, which is the innermost thing in a person, dearer than wealth, dearer than a son and dearer than everything else. It is only when a man regards his self as dear to him that what he holds dear will never perish. There are three worlds: the world of man to be obtained by a son; the world of the fathers, to be obtained by performing rites; and the world of the gods, to be obtained by knowledge. It goes on to state that as a spider sends forth its thread and as tiny sparks spring forth from a fire, so indeed does breath (prana), all the world and all the gods, and all beings spring from this self, the atman. It is the real behind the real. When at birth a person takes on a body, he becomes united with evil and when at death he leaves it behind, he gets rid of evil. Then again, we are told that atman/brahman is like salt when it dissolves in water and cannot be perceived. Yet, if a single sip is taken, the person who takes the sip knows that the salt is there.

This Upanishad is known for the description of brahman with the famous words '*Neti, neti*' 'not this, not this', for brahman cannot be understood empirically and has to be experienced (Chapter IV. 4.22; this is part of a long conversation between Yajnavalkya and King Janak of Videha). It is only by seeing and hearing oneself, and reflecting and concentrating on oneself, that one gains brahman. The Upanishad goes on to speak of atman being the honey, or *madhu*, or the inner essence of all things. It is immortal and it is everything. It is beyond hunger and thirst, sorrow and illusion, old age and death. It is the inner controller of all, who sees what cannot be seen, hears what cannot be heard, thinks what cannot be thought of, and perceives what cannot be perceived. One of the qualities of brahman is to be calm, composed and collected, not affected by evil or doubt.

Interestingly, this Upanishad contains one of the earliest formulations of the karma doctrine and clearly states that if a person's actions are good, he will become something good. If a person's actions are bad, he will become something bad. What happens to a person after he dies is stated, by Yajnavalkya, to depend entirely upon the karma or good action of that person before he dies. It describes how the atman leaves the body at death and takes up a new life, just like a caterpillar when it comes to the tip of a blade of grass, reaches out and draws something new to itself. The Upanishad speaks of the three cardinal ethical values of temperance, charity and compassion towards all living beings. Yajnavalkya asserts that brahman is the sum total of everything or 'everythingness' in the Universe. It is also stated to be the essence of everything, the madhuvidya or the honey within everything.

A large part of the Upanishad is conversations between persons. A conversation between King Ajatashatru and Balaki Gargya emphasizes the struggle to realize what is real. Yajnavalkya and his wife, Maitreya, speak of love and spirituality and state that ultimately true love is longing to attain the self as this alone represents what is real, and what is eternal bliss. Another conversation between Gargi and Yajnavalkya discusses philosophical ideas and the importance of seeking spiritual wisdom; that is, the quest to understand what is timeless and unchanging, what is real as opposed to what is not in this material world.

Isha Upanishad

The opening lines of the Isha Upanishad speak of Isha or Ishvar and say that everything that moves on Earth is enveloped by God. Renounce this world and enjoy thyself. Covet no wealth of any man. Karma, or one's deeds, cling to a person throughout his life, resulting in the person ignoring his true self or atman. In order to be liberated, the only way is to know yourself, which is motionless, yet faster than the mind, distant yet near, within all and without all, that which is all-pervading. He who beholds all beings in the self and the self in all beings attains the self. It is only when this realization dawns on a person and when this great unity is attained, that sorrow and trouble disappear.

This can only be done by the study of *vidya*, which is the study of eternal truths and not *avidya* or things which are mere empirical truths. One-sided pursuits lead to darkness; it is only when a person perceives and distinguishes between what is true and what is not that liberation and immortality take place. The Upanishad states that fire and mind lead a person to live a life of virtue and be away from a life of vice, so that he may be on the right path and may enjoy wealth as a result.

Taittiriya Upanishad

This Upanishad has three chapters: the Shikshavali, the Brahmanandvali and the Bhriguvali. The Shikshavali is the chapter dealing with instruction or education. It speaks of a lifelong pursuit of knowledge. A student has to recite that he will only speak what is right and true so that brahman may protect him and his teacher. The next verse asserts that a student must master the principles of phonetics as it is this alone which ensures that that which is transmitted from teacher to student for generations is accurately transmitted. The verse that follows speaks of how everything in the Universe is connected by this oral transmission from teacher to student. The sixth part of the Shikshavali asserts that atman, the self, exists, and when a person becomes the lord of his own mind, (speech, sight, hearing and perception), then he becomes brahman whose body is space and whose self is truth, whose pleasure ground is the life breath, or prana, and whose joy is the mind. The seventh *anuvaka,* or part of the Shikshavali states that everything in this world is five-fold and that there is a likeness between the microcosm and the macrocosm, and when a person understands this, the person becomes the macrocosm. The eighth anuvaka speaks of the word Om and asserts that though it is used for diverse purposes, it is really to remind us to celebrate brahman. The ninth anuvaka is important in that it deals with ethical truths and states that each ethical truth must first be a study of oneself after which there is study and discussion of the Vedas. Thus, justice, truth, penance, the giving up of desire, tranquillity, forgiveness, affability, hospitality, etc., must all be seen through these two lenses. And finally, a student is told never to go away from the truth, from dharma. Importantly, the practical wisdom of never neglecting one's well-being, health or prosperity, and never to neglect the continuous study of oneself and the Vedas is also emphasized. The graduating student finally acknowledges that these teachings have helped him and that his teacher is the visible brahman.

The second chapter, the Brahmanandvali, focuses on the realization of the self or atman. Brahman is described as the highest—it is truth, it is knowledge, and it is bliss. Knowledge seeking is then conceived in steps. The first is to meditate on the nature of food because food alone is the basis of life. After this, it is important to meditate on prana or life force, then the mind, then thought, and then knowledge and ethics. One ultimately comes to the hidden layer of existence, which is ultimate bliss, tranquillity and contentment. This is the realm of atman/ brahman characterized by love, joy, cheerfulness and bliss.

The third *vali* or the Bhriguvali speaks about the knowledge that a sage called Bhrigu obtained from his father, Varuni. This knowledge is of introspection and moving inwards to help arrive at the innermost kernel of knowledge of the self. The Upanishad again speaks about food and describes the cycle or chain of food which every living being is for other living beings. It states: 'The one who gives me, will indeed eat me. I am food and I eat him who eats food. It is then that I conquer the entire Universe and am like the light in the heavens.' Only when one knows this, one understands the hidden teaching of this Upanishad.

Katha Upanishad

This Upanishad is in two parts and begins with the story of Vajasrava who gives away all his worldly possessions. He has a son called Nachiketa who sees this giving away as a farce because what is actually given away is of no value to the recipients. The son then asks his father, 'To whom will you give me away?' and repeats it a second and a third time. The angry father replies, 'To Death, I will give you away.'

Nachiketa does not die but is sent to visit the abode of Yama, the God of Death. When he arrives, Yama is not in his abode. He remains there for three days and nights, after which Yama arrives. Yama apologizes and says Nachiketa may ask him for three boons for having kept him waiting for three days and nights. The first boon that he asks for is that be sent back to his family, especially to his father whose anger has vanished. This boon is granted immediately. He then goes on to ask for the proper execution of a fire ritual that enables a human being to get to heaven. Yama teaches him this ritual and then adds that anyone who does three kinds of rituals—performing the rituals themselves, studying the scriptures, and doing charity and understanding why he's doing it—will then become free from sorrow. The third boon that Nachiketa asks of Yama is to answer the question: 'What happens to a person after he dies?' Yama prevaricates in his answer and asks Nachiketa to ask for some other boon. Yama offers him worldly wealth and pleasure but Nachiketa wisely says that human life is short, and continues to ask the same question. In the second chapter, Yama gives a remarkable answer. He tells Nachiketa that one must distinguish between what is pleasant and what is good. He who chooses what is good will live on after death in happiness, as opposed to he who chooses what is merely pleasant. Both the good and the pleasant are choices, one difficult and one easy. It is only the wise who choose the good whereas it is the fool who chooses what is pleasant.

Atman is unborn and eternal. It can never be killed; if the killer thinks that he kills and the killed thinks that he is killed, neither understands. The atman is smaller than the small, greater than the great, and is hidden in the heart of each creature. It is free from avarice and grief, and is content and peaceful. It is therefore clear that the atman can only be obtained by persons whose conduct is ethical and whose mind is calm and tranquil.

In the third chapter, the Upanishad then goes on to speak of the parable of the chariot; atman is the rider in the chariot, the body is the chariot, intelligence, or *buddhi*, is the charioteer, and the mind is the reins. The senses are the horses, the objects of the senses are their paths and are formed out of the union of the atman, the senses and the mind. It is only those who use their mind, intelligence and reasoning in accordance with ethics that can ultimately reach atman.

The third chapter then speaks of a hierarchy beginning with *artha* or attainment of wealth, that is the object, above which is the senses, above which is the mind, above which is the intellect. It is above this intellect that there is atman or one's real self. And above this is *purusha,* or cosmic self. Beyond purusha, there is nothing. This is the very highest that one can attain. This can be done by self-restraint and by tempering the senses and the mind to the attainment of this great goal.

Part II, Chapter 1, asserts that inner knowledge is the knowledge of unity of the self in all living beings. The self is eternal—it is never born, and it never dies. To understand the eternal nature of one's own self is when externally there is calmness, patience and a feeling of complete freedom regardless of the circumstances that one is in or the threats or insults one faces. Inner peace and not sensory perception is what is stressed upon. And persons who know their self and act according to their dharma will remain pure, like pure water which remains pure when poured into an ocean of pure water.

Chapter 2 speaks of what happens to the self after death, and says that some of these selves enter wombs and become organic beings; others become immovable things according to their karma. The self is always awake and active even while one is asleep.

Chapter 3 tells us that beyond the senses is the mind; above the mind is intelligence; beyond intelligence is atman; and beyond atman is the unmanifest; beyond the unmanifest is cosmic man (purusha). One ought to know purusha in order to obtain eternal life. Only when the mind, its thoughts, and the five senses stand still, when buddhi, that is the intellect, does not waver (that is when the mind gets concentrated) that one is able to attain the knowledge of the yoga of creation and dissolution. Importantly, this state of perfection can be attained here and now for a person who knows that his atman is the cosmic self.

Shvetashvatara Upanishad

This Upanishad begins with metaphysical questions about the first cause. Is it time, nature, necessity, chance, matter or spirit? The self is itself powerless because independent of it there is a cause for good and evil. Through metaphors, the verse goes on to speak of a river whose water consists of five streams, whose waves are the five vital breaths, whose fountainhead is the mind. It has five whirlpools and its rapids are the five pains. It has fifty kinds of suffering and fifty branches. The text then points out that brahman is Ishvar or God. This Ishvar is eternal. And matter is divided into subject, object and the mover of matter. It is only when one meditates and realises that these three things are within the self that it dawns on one that all *pradhan* or matter is perishable and Hara or God is imperishable. It is only by meditating on God and becoming one with God that one is liberated from the cycle of birth and rebirth. The second chapter of this Upanishad extols yoga and its practice, both physical and mental, and describes the benefits of yoga to be agility, better health, a clear complexion, sweetness of voice, sweet odour, regular bodily functions and steadiness, all of which ultimately leads to the knowledge of the self.

The third chapter speaks of Isha or Rudra, who is the God who resides within. This chapter speaks of one God, Ekarudra, who is eternal and all pervading. This God is nothing but brahman who is the Creator of everything. Brahman is concealed in all beings and encompasses the entire Universe. It is formless and all pervading.

The fourth chapter contains an enigmatic verse that speaks of three unborn beings: one feminine and two masculine. There is one unborn being, the feminine, who is red, white and black, producing many creatures like herself. Then there is one unborn being, masculine, who loves her and stays with her. And there is another unborn being, masculine, who leaves her after loving her. Commentators have differed on the meaning of this verse. It seems that the reference is to the Samkhya doctrine of purusha and *prakriti* or matter and spirit.

Matter, that is prakriti, consists of three *guna*s which are *sattva, rajas* and *tamas* or purity, passion and ignorance. All creatures that are produced are a mix of these three gunas. The unborn being who loves prakriti is purusha or the cosmic self, and the unborn being who leaves her after loving her is the individual atma, or self. This chapter goes on to speak of how the individual self is caught up by maya, the cosmic self being the mind or the magician.

The fifth chapter describes brahman as being everywhere, the knowledge of which ultimately liberates a human being. It is described as not woman, not man; whatever body it takes, with that it is joined. The sixth chapter speaks of how persons speculate whether nature or time is the first cause of all things. It then declares that both these theories are wrong. It is God or Deva which is the first cause. God alone is the knower, the Creator of time, the Creator of nature and exists in all living creatures. This God is the self which is veiled inside men. Samkhya and yoga are said to be the means through which one can attain liberation by knowledge of God as being the primal cause.

The end of the Upanishad, in the sixth chapter, speaks of Deva and brahman/ atman interchangeably and says that Deva is the light of everything, who is self-made and the Supreme Spirit, the consciousness of those who are conscious and the master of both purusha and prakriti, the cause of transmigration. It is only a person who has the highest bhakti or love/ devotion to God and to his guru; to him who is high-minded, will these teachings be illuminating. The end of this Upanishad seems to emphasize that it is by the path of bhakti or devotion to God that one can reach God through the illuminating teachings of a guru who has realized God.

Maitraniya Upanishad

This Upanishad begins with the tale of a king named Brihadrath who renounces his kingdom and seeks the knowledge of the self. He goes to a sage called Sakayanya. The king, on being told that the seeking of this knowledge is extremely difficult, keeps on insisting that he be instructed. In the second chapter, the sage then asserts that knowledge of brahman and the knowledge contained in all the Upanishads was brought by a sage, Maitreya. The sage then narrates an ancient dialogue between Valakhilyas and Prajapati Kratu which states that man was created in the image of his Creator. He then goes on to say that Prajapati who is the lord of the creatures, divided himself and resides in a body made intelligent, the atman being the driver of the chariot, which is the body. Such persons experience the fruits of their karma and become one of the three gunas—sattva, rajas and tamas—which mean the highest or those who attain truth, the passionate and the ignorant. The self which is within is said to be pure, unchanging, unmoving and serenely calm. It is the spectator within oneself.

The third chapter speaks of human suffering and says that this occurs because of another different self called *bhutatma* or the ghost self which transmigrates. It is this self that suffers as a result of its karma and the complex interplay of the three gunas. The immortal self, however, is unaffected by all this. The fourth chapter then speaks of how this *bhut* self can obtain union with the true self, and the answer is that this is to acquire knowledge of the Vedas and perform one's duties ethically, and devote oneself to the stage of life in which one is. That is, in the first or *brahmacharya* stage, to be a good student; in the *grihastha,* to lead a good family life; in the third, *vanaprastha,* in which one is to prepare oneself to leave the world by living in the forest; and the fourth, *sanyas,* which is the seeking of the knowledge to liberate oneself. Interestingly, the worship of a particular God, be it Agni, Vayu or Brahma is only temporary because these deities that are meditated upon and worshipped must then be denied and dropped. It is on denial of these individual gods that unity takes place with the universal self.

In the fifth chapter, it states that the self is the hidden unchanging reality, the one without beginning or end. The three gunas which reside in everyone must give way to being sattvic only by ultimately reaching Vishnu, who is stated to be the sattva guna. In the sixth chapter, the self is stated to be within a human being and without. There are two parts: one inner and one outer. Man should meditate on both these selves with the symbol Om. The sixth chapter then speaks of the symbol Om, it being the light of the sun, the meditation on Om being the meditation on brahman/atman. The Gayatri Mantra is then referred to and explained, stating that when Savitri (the sun) is to inspire our thoughts, and stimulates our thoughts, what it really does is to teach us to meditate on the sun as worshipping the self. Yoga is then stated to be the best way in which to reach the self because it is through tranquillity of thought that all karma, good and evil, is destroyed and the self is attained. Interestingly, liberation is achieved through one's mind and one is told what a man thinks, that he becomes. This is how powerful the mind is.

In the seventh chapter, we are told that the self is the innermost being of everything that exists; it is tranquil, fearless, sorrowless and indescribable joy; it is Vishnu, it is Shivam, it is Aditya, it is Indra. The Upanishad ends by stating that it is important not to follow teachings of persons who deny the self, and other persons who beg, preach hedonism and who are really rogues masquerading as religious mendicants. These false teachers should be abjured. The end of this Upanishad may well be a counter to the teachings of the Buddhists and the Charvakas, which have been described in this book as well.

Mandukya Upanishad

This is a short Upanishad which speaks about the qualities of Om. It opens by declaring that Om is the entire world and that time is three-fold—past, present, and future—and all three are Om. That which transcends time is what is beyond Om and that is brahman. The Upanishad then speaks of four states of consciousness. The first is the waking state in which we are aware of the world around us. The second is the mind which produces dreams in our sleep. The third is a state of undistracted or deep sleep. And the fourth is that which transcends these three states of consciousness, and it is this state that is said to be *chitta* or *anand* or complete bliss. 'Om' is split into three syllables: AUM. The syllable 'a' symbolically is our waking state, 'u' is the mind with dreams, and 'm' is the mind when it is in deep sleep, and that which transcends these is complete bliss.

Mundaka Upanishad

This Upanishad begins by stating that the knowledge of brahman is the foundation of all knowledge and then lists a number of teachers who share this knowledge with their pupils by name. It then goes on to speak of a discussion between Angiras, who is the teacher, and Saunaka, the person who is seeking this knowledge. The question asked is: 'What is that through which if it is known, everything else becomes known?' Angiras' answer begins by classifying knowledge into lower and higher knowledge. Lower knowledge includes knowledge of the Vedas, grammar, astrology, sacrifice, rituals, etc. Higher knowledge is the means by which one can comprehend what is imperishable, that is the knowledge of brahman. The analogy of a spider, plants and hair is then given by the Upanishad as follows: Just as a spider spins out and holds the threads of its web, just as plants sprout forth out of the Earth, and just as hair grows on the head of a man who lives, similarly, everything else arises out of the imperishable one.

Then comes the famous passage in which sacrifices and the study of the Vedas is stated to be foolish because it leads again and again to old age and death, as such persons dwell in darkness, wise in their own conceit and puffed up with vanity. They are indeed blind men, being led by the blind. The spiritual knowledge that leads to brahman and liberates man can only be through *tapas,* that is penance, and by living a simple and tranquil life, preferably on alms and without any ritual or sacrifice. Acts which themselves are perishable obviously cannot lead to knowledge of what is eternal.

The second chapter of this Upanishad then speaks of how brahman is imperishable, without body, all pervading, and self-existent. It states that brahman is in fact the cause of everything that exists, having never been created itself. It then states that since brahman is beyond sensory perception,

it can only be known through an intellect that is purified
by spiritual knowledge and meditation and not by a mere
reading of the Vedas. It is this alone that leads to brahman.
Meditation on Om is one excellent way in which to reach
perfect bliss.

The third chapter speaks of the famous allegory of two
birds. It says two birds who were inseparable friends clung
to the same tree. One of them ate the fruit on the tree and
the other simply looked around without eating. On the same
tree sat a man in grief, bewildered and helpless. It was only
when he saw himself as isa and purusha who had their source
in brahman, that he became wise and reached the eternal
and transcendental self. These two birds appear to refer to
the individual soul that is imprisoned in man, atman, and
the man of sensory perception.

The Upanishad ends by asserting that ethics is necessary
for a man to obtain knowledge of the self, and ethics is
divided into satya, that is truth, tapas, that is penance,
samyajnana, that is correct knowledge and *brahmacharya*
which is celibacy or abstinence. This knowledge can never be
achieved by sensory perception or by rituals. The Upanishad
states that the self cannot be realized by those who lack
inner strength, are careless or are devoted to false notions
of austerity. Once the self is sought, it reveals its own truth.
Once it is obtained, the mind becomes calm. And the life
of liberation emerges in which the person who has reached
brahman is beyond sorrow and beyond sin, as such a person
is in union with the self.

Prashna Upanishad

This is the Upanishad which contains six questions, all of which are answered by Sage Pippalada. When students want the sage to give them answers to these questions, the sage begins by stating that the answers will only become meaningful if the students first live with their gurus for a year, with tapas, brahmacharya and satya, that is with penance, meditation, celibacy and true devotion.

The first question that is asked of the sage is: 'How are living beings created?' The answer given is that Prajapati, the Lord of the Creatures performed tapas (that is penance) and then created the female principle, that is matter, and the male principle, that is spirit, referred to as *rayi* and prana. These together then produced living beings. After this question is answered, it is stated that it is important for persons who wish to realize atman/ brahman to live a life of satya, that is truth, brahmacharya, that is control over sexual desires, tapas or austerity and no *jihma* (meaning intent not to do the right thing), no *anritam* (falsehood) and no *maya* (here meaning guile).

The second question goes on to ask how many devas or gods uphold a living being and who is the best of them. The answer given by the sage is that the five gross elements, the five senses, the five organs, etc., are all expressions of deities and the best of them is prana, which is breath or spirit, because without breath nothing else can exist in a living being.

The third question is then subdivided into six questions: How is life born? When born, does it come into the body?

When it has entered the body, how does it reside there? How does it go out of the body? How does life generally interact with nature and the senses? And finally, how does life interact with the self? The sage states that these questions are difficult to answer but then answers them by saying that it is from atman or the unsullied self that a human being is born in this life. Life enters the body by an act of mind and governs the body by delegating work to the other organs. The Upanishad then gives an account of the human body which has the heart as its principal organ from which arise 101 major arteries, each then subdivided into smaller and smaller arteries, which then diffuse air throughout the body. It is this life breath which ultimately gives or sustains life in a human being.

The fourth question is: What sleeps in man? What is awake in man when he sleeps? Which God in man is it that sees dreams? What is it in man that experiences happiness and ultimately, on what is all this founded? The answer begins by reciting that all sensory organs withdraw and become one with the highest God named mind as man sleeps. It is then pointed out that prana, or breath, never sleeps. Dream is a form of recreation for the mind because it goes into activities which are in the past, maybe in this life or in another, maybe true or untrue, pleasant or unpleasant; in a dream the mind beholds everything. When the mind falls into a deep sleep state without any dreams, complete relaxation and happiness ensue as the person who is so asleep retires back into atman/brahman. Finally, the sage says that all of this is founded in the supreme, indestructible self and it is only when one returns to this state that bliss, eternal bliss can be attained.

The fifth question is, if a human being sincerely meditates on Om until he is dead, what would he obtain? The answer given is interesting. It says that if a person meditates on the first letter of Om that is 'a', it will lead to a quick rebirth but only for a person who is ethically inclined. If a person meditates on 'a' and 'u', the intermediate level, then, such a person will undoubtedly enjoy life in heaven after which he is reborn in the world of man. But it is only the person who meditates on all the aspects of the self, that is all the three syllables of 'a', 'u' and 'm' who gets liberated from all suffering and birth and death because such a person has then reached brahman.

The sixth question speaks of a prince who visits a student and asks, 'Where is the person with sixteen parts?' The student confesses that he doesn't know. Sage Pippalada answers stating that every human being has sixteen parts just like the Creator Prajapati, as man is created in Prajapati's image. It is when this becomes known to man that he becomes one with the self that is immortal.

Bhagavad Gita

We now come to the culmination of the Upanishadic thought in the Bhagavad Gita. This remarkable text is in eighteen chapters and occurs in the Bhishma Parva, the sixth book of the Mahabharata. Though described as an Upanishad, it is not linked with any one of the Vedas. Many contradictory strains found in the Upanishads are sought to be reconciled in the Bhagavad Gita. For example, does the reading of the Vedas lead to liberation? How are heaven and hell and reincarnation possible together? Do women, Shudras and outcastes also attain liberation? Have purusha and prakriti always existed or were they created by God? And above all, do we worship a personal God in order to reach liberation, or is it the spiritual knowledge that leads to brahman that gets us liberation? The Bhagavad Gita or the Song of the Lord is an exposition of Upanishadic thought given by Lord Krishna who is believed to be Lord Vishnu's incarnation or *avatar* on Earth. According to the epic, Arjuna, one of the five Pandavas, is about to begin fighting a fratricidal war against his cousins, his teacher Dronacharya, and various other persons he has grown up with. Chapter 1 begins with his hesitancy and despondency. Arjun tells Krishna, who is his charioteer, that he wishes to put down his bow and does not wish to fight as he might kill his elders and his cousins.

The Bhagavad Gita is an emanation from the mouth of the Lord himself, not only as to how Arjun should conduct himself in the war, but what happens to man in life and in the afterlife. It is therefore a complete exposition of ethics and metaphysics as understood in the Upanishads. Chapter 2, about Samkhya theory and Yoga practice, refers to two Hindu philosophical schools, Samkhya and Yoga, which will be discussed in more detail later in this book. Samkhya is essentially an atheistic school with the belief that purusha and prakriti, that is spirit and matter, are

eternal and that there is no God who created the Universe.
It is the knowledge of the difference between purusha and
prakriti that ultimately leads to liberation. Yoga, which
is also a philosophical school, however, believes in Ishvar
or a personal God, who is the Creator of everything. The
realization of purusha and prakriti can be had by fixing one's
mind on the Supreme Lord and yearning for deliverance and
by various physical practices that conduce to an ultimately
spiritual state of being.

Chapter 2 tells us a number of truths. In Verse 16, it
states, 'Of that which is non-existent, there will be no coming
to be and of that which is existent there is no ceasing to be.'
In Verse 17, it tells us that brahman is indestructible; Verse
27 says that those who are wise do not grieve because death
is certain and so is rebirth for the human being who dies. In
Verse 31, Arjun is exhorted to do battle as that is the duty
of every Kshatriya—a person who belongs to the Kshatriya
varna or class of warriors. He is then told in Verse 37, that if
he does his duty as a warrior, he can never lose. If he is slain,
he will go to heaven and if he is victorious, he will enjoy life
on Earth. The chapter then goes on to speak of the Vedas
and their study. In Verse 42, we are told that their study will
lead to bewilderment (Verse 53) and it is only when one's
intelligence stands unshaken and stable that one will get
insight to become a true yogi. We are then told in Verse 47
that come what may, one cannot escape from action. What
is, therefore, important is to realize this, and to give up any
attachment to the fruits of action and give up any thoughts

of inaction. However, we are further cautioned in Verse 49, that action itself is far inferior to the knowledge that will ultimately lead to liberation. Control the senses and be intent on attaining God (Verse 61). Never forget that from attachment springs desire, from desire springs anger, from anger springs bewilderment, from bewilderment, springs loss of memory and from loss of memory springs destruction of intelligence (Verses 62 and 63).

In Chapter 3, entitled 'Karma Yoga', we are told of one of the three paths to attain God and this is the path of action or duty. We are reminded again that no one can remain without action and that therefore, if one's duty is done without attachment, or without any expectation of reward, only then will one attain the highest (Verses 5 and 19). We are reminded that God himself works all the time, otherwise there would be chaos in the Universe (Verse 24). We are then told that greater than the senses is the mind, greater than the mind is intelligence, and greater than intelligence is God. Know and experience the Almighty who is beyond intelligence (Verses 42 and 43).

Chapter 4 speaks of the way of knowledge. Knowledge and wisdom are extolled and ignorance decried. We are told that many past lives have occurred before we have reached this life. Krishna then says that whenever there is a decline of righteousness on Earth, God comes in order to save this Earth (Verse 7). God is beyond action or change, being perfect. It is He who has created the four varnas, that is the four classes into which society was then divided: the Brahmin or the priest, the Kshatriya or the warrior, the Vaishya, the trader or merchant, and the Shudra, the person who serves the other three (Verse 13). He who sees action in inaction and inaction in action is wise and is a true yogi (Verse 18). Ever content, such a person abandons attachment to the fruit of his actions and gives up his possessions (Verses 20 and 21). He is also satisfied with whatever comes his way (Verse 22). The gaining of knowledge as a sacrifice is itself the greatest sacrifice (Verse 33). It is by wisdom alone that even sinners will ultimately get over evil and attain the ultimate (Verse 36). On the other hand, those who are ignorant, that is, those who do not have faith and are of a doubting nature, will undoubtedly perish (Verse 40).

Chapter 5 speaks of true renunciation. It says that between the renunciation of the fruits of work and the unselfish performance of work, the latter is better (Verse 2) but both paths ultimately will lead to the same goal (Verse 5). Importantly, sages realize that all men are equal; even an outcast can attain the same goal (Verse 18). Pleasure born of sense perception has a beginning and an end and therefore, inevitably leads to sorrow (Verse 22). Happiness can only come from within. Once this is realized, one attains God (Verse 24).

Chapter 6 speaks of the true yogi. The self is both a friend and a foe because a man has to lift himself only by himself; nobody else can do this for him (Verse 5). It is only when a clod of earth, a stone and gold are all the same to a person that he can be said to have attained the yoga state (Verse 8). Such a person is neutral and impartial to saints and sinners alike, as he has gone beyond the dualities in nature (Verse 9). Celibacy, serenity and fearlessness are a result of a mind which is fixed on God, and therefore attains God (Verse 14). Yoga is a middle path. Remember, never to overeat or oversleep (Verse 16). The true yogi sees God everywhere (Verse 30). And a true yogi is greater than an ascetic, a man of knowledge or a man who performs rituals (Verse 46).

Chapter 7 speaks of God and the world, and is an emphatic affirmation of theism. It begins by stating that of the thousands of persons that exist, only one strives for perfection and of those who strive only one knows God (this is how difficult the path of knowledge is). Krishna then tells us: 'I am the origin and dissolution of this world' (Verse 6). There is nothing higher than God (Verse 7). Evil is ignorance and foolishness (Verse 15). Of those who are virtuous, there are four kinds. Those who are in distress because they seek virtue, those who seek wealth, those who seek knowledge and the man of wisdom. The man of wisdom is undoubtedly the best of the lot (Verses 16 and 17). On the other hand, those whose minds are distorted by desire resort to worshipping other gods and believe in rites and rituals. Such persons who worship other gods go to those other gods; temporary is their visit. On the other hand, those who are devoted to me, come only to me (Verses 20 and 23). In an explanation of what God is, he states: 'I am unborn, unchanging and omniscient. I know the past, the present and the future but nobody knows me' (Verses 25 and 26).

In Chapter 8, titled 'The Course of Cosmic Evolution', we are told that whoever thinks of God at the time of death goes to Him. The best way to attain God is to utter and meditate upon Om because that is how one attains brahman (Verses 5 and 13). Once a person has attained this, there will be no rebirth (Verse 15). One day of brahman is equal to a thousand ages; so is one night of brahman a thousand ages (Verse 17).

Chapter 9 is titled 'God is More than His Creation'. All beings abide in God, but not God in them (Verse 4). It is only under God's guidance that nature gives birth to living beings (Verse 10). God is all; God is the ritual, the sacrifice, the father, the mother, the good, the bad (Verses 16 to 18). God is immortality and death, being and non-being (Verse 19). Now comes the interesting coupling of reincarnation, with heaven. We are told that those who study and live according to the three Vedas reach heaven, enjoy the pleasure of the gods until their merit is exhausted, and then they come back to Earth as a reincarnated being (Verses 20 and 21). We are also informed that devotees of other gods in reality sacrifice to the one God alone, though not correctly (Verse 23). God accepts any offering with a pure heart as nothing is hateful or dear to God (Verses 26 and 29). Even a man of the vilest conduct who worships God is said to be righteous, for he has resolved correctly, albeit ultimately (Verse 30). Importantly, the Bhagavad Gita was a progressive text when it was composed, as women and Shudras also attain God if they practise what is written here (Verse 32).

In Chapter 10, God is stated to be the source of everything. To know Him, is to know everything. We are reminded that God is unborn and has no beginning (Verse 3). It is out of compassion that the darkness of ignorance is destroyed by the wisdom of light (Verse 11). Between Verses 20 and 42, God describes how He is everything. Verse 34 is important because it says, 'I am Death, the all devouring and the origin of things that are yet to be'. This verse is known as the 'Oppenheimer verse' because this is what Robert Oppenheimer referred to when the atom bomb was created, referring to the atom bomb's effects.

Chapter 11 speaks of God's transfiguration. Arjun is given a special eye with which to see the true nature of God by which he beholds the Universe. He sees the light of a thousand suns, sees 'everything', that is, no beginning, no middle, no end and men going to their destruction and others being born. Arjun is dazed by this and begs the Lord to give him back his ordinary sight.

Chapter 12 speaks of the worship of Ishvar, the personal God, being better than the meditation on an impersonal brahman. Knowledge is better than concentration, better than knowledge is meditation, and better than meditation is the renunciation of the fruits of action (Verse 12). We are told not to shrink from the world so that the world does not shrink from us. Be free from joy, anger and fear, for if you are not a source of grief, no grief will come to you (Verse 15). And we are reminded that whoever denounces dualities, good and evil, and neither rejoices nor hates, neither grieves nor desires, will undoubtedly go back to God.

Chapter 13 speaks of the field and the knower of the field, matter and the soul, and the difference between them. This chapter deals with Samkhya theory, which is the difference between spirit and matter. We are told that we are made up of five elements, ten senses and the mind (Verse 5). It is important to practise humility, integrity, non-violence, patience, purity and self-control in order to know brahman (Verses 7 and 12). Brahman dwells in the world enveloping everything (Verse 13). It is the unmoved mover, far yet near, subtle at all times (Verse 15). Purusha and prakriti are both beginningless (Verse 19; this verse seemingly contradicts the teaching of the Gita that everything has a beginning and the source is Almighty God). We are then told that if we have the knowledge of purusha and prakriti and the three natures—sattva (goodness), tamas (passion) and rajas (ignorance)—and bring ourselves to a sattvic nature, we will attain God. We are then told that by meditation, we can perceive the self, in the self, by the self. There are three paths to God: the path of knowledge, or *jnanayoga*; the path of duty or *karmayoga*; and the path of devotion, or *bhaktiyoga*—all leading to God (Verses 24 and 25).

Chapter 14 speaks of God as being the mystical father of all beings. This chapter speaks of the three natures of man: sattva, rajas and tamas. We are told that sattva is illumination and health (Verse 6), rajas is craving and attachment (Verse 7), and tamas is ignorance (Verse 8). Goodness attaches one to happiness, passion to action, and dullness or ignorance to negligence (Verse 9). Hence, there are three kinds of rebirths. A sattvic person is reborn in the Brahmalok, or the abode of the gods; a rajasic person is reborn in the womb of those who are attached to action; and a tamasic person is reborn in the womb of those who are deluded (Verse 15). He who is above all the three and constant in all things alone can reach God (Verse 24).

It is important at this stage to go to Chapter 17 as the three natures are again spoken of, this time as applied to religious phenomena. This chapter states that sattvic people worship gods, rajasic people worship demons, and tamasic people worship spirits and ghosts (Verse 4). Violent austerity is bad; it is impelled by vanity, conceit, lust and passion (Verse 5). Food also is of three kinds: sattvic food being nourishing, rajasic food being bitter and sour, and tamasic food being putrid and stale (Verses 8–10). A sattvic sacrifice is good because there is no expectation of reward (Verse 11). A rajasic sacrifice expects a reward and is done for the sake of display. A tamasic sacrifice has no hymns, no food and is totally devoid of faith (See Verses 11–13). Penance done without expectation of reward is sattvic. Penance here means non-violent conduct, speech which is truthful and which gives no offence, and a mind which controls the senses and is serene and gentle. Penance, in order to show off, is rajasic and penance by which one mortifies or injures oneself or others is tamasic (see Verses 17–19). Likewise, gifts that are given without expectation of return, with expectation of return, or given at the wrong time or place, or to unworthy persons are sattvic, rajasic and tamasic, respectively.

Chapter 15 speaks of the Tree of Life and states that the peepal tree has leaves which are the Vedas. The tree itself is God (Verse 1). In Verse 6, we are told that the sun and the moon only illuminate our abode, they have nothing to do with, and do not illuminate, the abode in which God lives.

Chapter 16 speaks of the nature of a god-like and a demonic mind, respectively. A god-like mind has the following qualities: fearlessness, purity, charity, self-control, study of scriptures, austerity, uprightness, non-violence, truth, absence of anger, aversion to fault finding, compassion to all living beings, gentleness, modesty, steadfastness, vigour, forgiveness, fortitude and freedom from malice, and pride (see Verses 1–3). The opposite is a demonic mind: ostentation, arrogance, pride, anger, harshness, ignorance, self-conceit, obstinacy, the arrogance of wealth, lust, anger and greed (see Verses 4, 17 and 21). We are assured that such persons are reborn in the wombs of demons (Verse 19). We are then told that in order to follow what should be done and what ought to and ought not to be done in living life requires a knowledge of the scriptures (Verse 24).

Chapter 18 speaks of the yoga of release by renunciation of the fruits of action. We are told that sacrifice, gifts and penance are purifiers of those who are wise. Perform and do them, but give up any attachment to doing them and any desire for their fruits. This is God's final view of the best method in which to reach Him (Verses 5 and 6). There must be no renunciation of any duty that ought to be done (Verse 7). There should be no aversion to disagreeable action and no attachment to agreeable action (Verse 10). Knowledge by which God is seen in all, is knowledge by sattvic pursuits. Knowledge by which God is seen only in certain beings is knowledge which is rajasic. And knowledge which is ignorant is where one sees one thing in everything without regard to what is real and is tamasic (Verses 20–22). When a person truly understands the self, happiness is like poison at first and then nectar. The exact reverse is when the person does not understand the self but is within the realm of pleasure and pain (Verses 37 and 38). And that happiness which deludes is from sloth and negligence (Verse 39). We are then given the four varnas and their natural qualities: the Brahmin is serene, has self-control, is pure, upright and wise; the Kshatriya is heroic, vigorous, does not flee from difficulties, is generous and is a leader; the Vaishya engages in agriculture and trade, and the Shudra does service to the others (see Verses 42–46). Worship God, therefore, through the performance of duty (Verse 46). We are reminded that it is better to do your own duty badly than to do another varna's duty perfectly (Verse 47). We are then told that he who dwells in solitude, eats little and meditates on God, reaches God (Verse 52). Ultimately it is by divine grace that one reaches the eternal, undying abode (Verse 56). It is by grace that all difficulties vanish if one's thought is fixed only on God (Verse 58). It is important not to state this to people who do not understand. It is only when this is studied and listened to that the 'sacrifice' of knowledge actually takes place, liberation being the outcome.

The Six Astika* Schools of Hindu Philosophy

Samkhya

This is an old and dualistic school of Hindu philosophy which believes that there is no God and that purusha and prakriti have existed eternally. Purusha is stated to be spirit, which is absolutely independent, beyond perception and indescribable. Prakriti, on the other hand, is stated to consist of matter as well as the human mind, which in turn consists of three gunas: sattva, that is the pure or unsullied; rajas, that is the passionate; and tamas, which is the ignorant. It is an admixture of these three gunas within prakriti that gets disturbed when purusha comes into contact with it.

There are many purushas which are floating around in the Universe. It is important to remember that in this

---

* 'Astika' means those schools that believe in the Vedas as authentic scriptural knowledge.

school of thought, there is no one universal spirit. Twenty-four tattvas make up a jiva, or soul, which is a combination of purusha with prakriti. They consist of the intellect, the ego, the mind, the five senses, five action capacities, five subtle elements such as form, sound, smell, taste, touch, and the five gross elements which are earth, fire, air, water and space. This school believes that only three *pramanas*, or thought processes, are valid: the first is *pratyaksha* which is perception, both external and internal; the second is *anumana* which is inferential thinking, and the third is *shabda* which is the word of the sages in scripture.

The actual word 'samkhya' means numbers, and the idea is generally to reach the twenty-fifth tattva, or number, which is none other than purusha itself. Ignorance is the cause of suffering and bondage, and it is correct knowledge that leads to moksha, or ultimate liberation. This knowledge is said to be a discernment of the difference between purusha and prakriti, and the means of liberation is to know how then to liberate oneself from prakriti and become purusha so that the jiva goes back to its original pure and pristine state.

The Samkhya doctrine speaks of three kinds of suffering: that which arises from the body, that which arises from the external world and that which is supernatural. It explicitly states that the Vedas are *shruti,* that which has been remembered and passed down orally through the ages and are worthy of study. However, Samkhya states that Ishvar cannot be proved logically. If the desire of one God was the beginning of the process of Creation, then there can be no God because God cannot have any desire. Equally, a perfect God does not exist since the created world is full of suffering. Otherwise God would have made the world perfect. Therefore, purusha, prakriti and karma—which is the law by which all living beings transmigrate—exist by themselves. The founder of this school is said to be Kapila, who lived in the sixth century BCE.

Yoga

This is the second great Hindu philosophical school and is to be practised along with Samkhya theory. This school is grounded in the *Yoga Sutras* of Patanjali who lived in the second century BCE. These sutras are 196 aphorisms which are found in four books. The eight basic elements of yoga in order to reach moksha, or liberation, are abstinence, observance of yoga's norms, *asanas*, which are physical exercises, *pranayama,* which is breath control, the withdrawal of the senses into the mind, concentration on the absolute Godhead through meditation, and finally, the reaching of samadhi, or the reaching of God. This is the path of Raja Yoga, so described by Swami Vivekananda. Unlike Samkhya, Yoga believes in Ishvar that is a personal God who is the unmoved mover of the Universe. True knowledge is stated to be the knowledge of the difference between purusha and prakriti, which when combined with yoga practices, both mental and physical, will ultimately lead to moksha.

The *Yoga Sutras* are divided into four *padas*, or chapters. The first is the Samadhi Pada, which consists of fifty-one sutras. This is the main technique by which the isolation of the mind from the impurities that it contains, is attained. This pada mentions seven different practices to still the mind, the seventh being meditation. The second chapter, Sadhana Pada, consists of fifty-five sutras and deals with different kinds of yoga. Kriya Yoga is a preparation stage for Ashtanga Yoga, which is the eight-limbed yoga and consists of austerity, a study of the scriptures and devotion to God. Ashtanga Yoga, or the yoga of eight limbs, speaks first of *yama*, which is restrained ethical behaviour. Yama, in turn, consists of non-violence, non-stealing, chastity and the giving up of desire. The second limb, *niyama*, which translated means observances, speaks of cleanliness, contentment, austerity, study of the scriptures by oneself and devotion to God. The third limb speaks of asana, which refers to physical postures through which the mind can be steadied. The fourth is pranayama, which is the control of one's breath. The fifth is *pratyahara*, which is the withdrawal of the senses into the mind. The sixth is *dharna*, or concentration. The seventh is *dhyana*, or meditation, and the eighth and ultimate limb is samadhi, which is reaching moksha, or liberation of the soul.

The third pada called the Vibhuti Pada, is a chapter which deals with empowering oneself to reach the goal. Here again there are fifty-six sutras in which by concentration and meditation, one gains an insight into purusha (which is pure spirit) and that can then give the yogi super-natural powers. This chapter, however, warns the yogi not to use these powers as they can become an obstacle to ultimately gaining liberation.

The fourth chapter, Kaivalya Pada, is the means of isolating the mind from its impure contents, so that it stands rock still and is ready for moksha. This pada consists of thirty-four sutras and asks the incumbent to essentially reflect on the various stages already gone through so that the difference between purusha and prakriti, combined with yogic practices, leads to ultimate liberation. This school which believes in a personal God, Ishvar, defines Ishvar as a special purusha that is a special or extraordinary spirit.

Nyaya School

This school of Hindu philosophy is a school of rules which believes in logic. It speaks of the Vedas as being important to instruct a person in the rules of behaviour and philosophy. It believes in four pramanas as opposed to Samkhya Yoga's three, adding *upamana* to the first three, which is comparison as a means of thought. This school states that suffering is due to wrong knowledge, that is delusion and ignorance. The Nyaya sutras are attributed to one Akshapada Gautama who is supposed to have lived between the sixth and second centuries BCE. Nyaya metaphysics recognizes sixteen categories of reasoning. These are:

pramana, that is a valid means of knowledge; *prameya*, the objects of such knowledge; *samshaya* meaning doubt;

prayojana meaning aim;

drishtanta meaning example;

siddhanta meaning accepted position; *avayava*, that is inferential components; *tarka*, that is hypothetical reasoning; *nirnaya*, that is certainty;

vaad, that is discussion or debate;

jalpa, that is wrangling;

vitanda, that is debate with an idea to confuse; *hetvabhasa*, that is fallacious reasoning; *chala*, which is quibbling;

jati, which is futile reasoning;

nigrahasthana, which is the point of defeat in a debate.

The theory of logic that Nyaya propounds is that for every proposition there needs to be proof, and for proof, there must be reason. Inference is regarded as one means of attaining truth. And after a particular proposition is laid down, it is important to go through the first few steps and reaffirm the proposition before one comes to a final conclusion. Causes and effects are very important. There are said to be three types of causes: the material cause, such as the thread in a piece of cloth; second, the non-material cause or the colour of the cloth; and third, the efficient cause that is the weaver of the cloth.

Strongly opposed to the Samkhya theory that God does not exist, Udayan, in his Nyaya *kumanjali* gave nine arguments to prove the existence of a Creator God. The first is that since the world is an effect and all effects must have an efficient cause, that efficient cause has to be God. Second, for atoms to combine, there has to be an intelligence which combines them and that intelligence has to be God. Third, whatever sustains and destroys in this world must again be due to intelligence and that intelligence is God. Fourth, the representational power of words, that is, every word has a meaning and represents an object, is to be found only in God. Fifth, since the Vedas are infallible and human beings are fallible, the author of the Vedas must be God. Sixth, the Vedas testify to the existence of God. Seventh, the Vedas deal with morals. These are divine injunctions and can only come from a divine creator of law. That divine Creator is God. Eighth, the ability to perfectly conceive concepts must be akin to something and that something is divine consciousness. Therefore, God must exist. And ninth, and most importantly, the doctrine of karma. Everybody reaps the fruits of his own actions, and an unseen power keeps a balance sheet of good and evil. This unseen power is God.

Vaisheshika School

The Vaisheshika School, often paired with the Nyaya School of Hindu philosophy, is otherwise called the atomist school. Unlike the other three schools we have spoken of, this one believes in only two types of pramanas, or thought: perception and inference. It was founded by one Kannada Kashyap who lived between the sixth and second centuries BCE. It speaks of the indivisible atom and states that all substances are composed of these atoms, namely earth, air, fire, water and space. This school states that all things that exist can be understood as objects which we experience.

It then speaks of the categories within which these objects of experience can be derived. The first is *dravya,* or substance. These are nine—earth, water, fire, air, aether, time, space, atman, the self and the mind. The second consists of gunas, or qualities. There are seventeen gunas according to the Vaisheshika Sutra. The seventeen qualities spoken of include colour, taste, smell, touch, number, size, individuality, accompaniment, disjunction, priority, posteriority, knowledge, pleasure, pain, desire, aversion and effort. To these are added weight, fluidity, viscosity, merit, demerit, sound and faculty. The third *padarth* is stated to be karma. Karma here means activity, and karma has no separate existence but is a quality which is a permanent feature of a particular substance. The karmas spoken of are aether, time, space and atman (self). The fourth padarth is stated to be samanya, or generality. The fifth is the opposite, that is *vishesha,* meaning particularity, through which persons are able to perceive differences in substances. And the sixth is *samavaaya* which is cause and effect.

Atoms are stated to be of four kinds: two which have mass and two which do not have mass. Each substance consists of all four kinds of atoms and each atom possesses its own particular individuality. Importantly, this school believes that each atom has existed eternally. God, therefore, has not created these atoms. But God exists as the unseen prime mover who arranges these atoms so that the Universe and everything in it is then created by God.

Purvamimamsa

The fifth school of Hindu philosophy is a school called Purvamimamsa. This again is an early school founded by Jaimini in 300 BCE and is atheistic. Several reasons are given by Kumarila Bhatta, a proponent of this school, as to why God does not exist. This school believes that the cycle of karma is perpetual. There can be no moksha or release from this cycle. The only thing one can aspire to is a life in heaven, if sacrifices are performed according to Vedic rites. Like Samkhya Yoga, only three pramanas or thought processes are valid, until Prabhakar and Kumarila added three more. The Vedas are said to be eternal. There is no particular authorship that can be ascribed to them. The atman or soul is distinct from the body and is in the mind; the Universe is real. There is a strict ritualistic basis to this school in which Vedic injunctions have to be followed to the tee. It is only then that one's dharma is realised. This school also says that it's only the first three varnas that can study the Vedas and perform sacrifices. Shudras cannot do so.

Vedanta

We now come to the sixth school of philosophy which is the Vedanta School. This school, which is closely related to both Shaivism and Vaishnavism, has three sources: the Upanishads; the Brahmasutras, which were composed much later so as to explain the Upanishads; the Bhagavad Gita and the Bhagavata Purana. The most famous school within Vedanta is the school of Adi Shankaracharya or the school known as the Advaita. Advaita stands for monism or the fact that nothing exists except brahman which is 'everythingness' and is all encompassing. The reason why a person cannot understand brahman is because of avidya, or ignorance. Maya, which is the appearance of things and not things as they really exist, is what bewilders human beings. The only reality is brahman.

Unfortunately, due to avidya, we take the world as it exists to be a reality. This school speaks of the atman, or the self, being covered by five layers, which are described as the food layer, the life-force layer, the mental layer, the discernment or wisdom layer and finally, once these layers are removed, *ananda,* or bliss, the fifth and innermost layer is attained, as a result of the merger with brahman.

Knowledge alone leads to liberation. The attainment of knowledge can only be from the study of the scriptures, proper reasoning and meditation on brahman. Four qualities are needed for an advaita student to be able to study the scriptures and reason properly. First, one must have the ability to discriminate between what is real and eternal, and that which is apparently real and not eternal. Second, one must renounce sense pleasures. Third, one must inculcate six important qualities: first, the ability to keep the mind in focus; second, to restrain the senses; third, to be dispassionate; fourth to be enduring and persevering in attaining brahman in a world of opposites; fifth, to have complete faith in one's guru and the shruti scriptural texts; and sixth, to be content. The fourth quality is perhaps the most important, which is an intense longing for moksha or liberation.

Three things are said to destroy avidya, or ignorance. One is to hear, literally, the scriptures. The second is to reflect on such teachings. And the third is to introspect with them, so that one reaches a stage of non-duality. The guru is important in order to share his experience with his students so as to reach moksha.

The second important school within Vedanta is referred to as Vishishtadvaita, or qualified monism. Its chief exponent was a sage called Ramanuja, who lived in the eleventh century CE. According to him, the self (atman) and brahman (the Universal Spirit) may ultimately be one as all diversity stems from a fundamental underlying unity, but otherwise atman is separate from but dependent on brahman. And one must believe in brahman as the God Vishnu is *saguna* brahman (the brahman that can be grasped by the mind) as opposed to *nirguna* brahman, that which cannot be grasped by the mind. Ramanuja differs with Shankaracharya in that according to him, the path to reach Vishnu is bhakti, or the path of love for a personal God, and not the path of knowledge. Ramanuja believed in the underlying unity of all souls, in which the atman ultimately experiences the same bliss as brahman.

Yet another school of Vedanta is the Dvaita school of Madhavacharya, who loved in the thirteenth century. Madhavacharya said brahman and atman are different and retain their differences throughout time. Bhakti yoga is prescribed as the means of reaching God. Atman is different from brahman and enjoys chitta, ananda or bliss differently from the bliss of the universal spirit.

In the seventh century CE, Bheda-abheda or Dvaita-advaita was advocated by a sage called Nimbarka. According to this school of thought, both spirit and matter are real. Krishna, an avatar of Vishnu, is the cause of the Universe and the teaching of this school is to get back to Krishna through meditation and devotion. This school of thought, therefore, advocates a combination of gyan and bhakti yoga.

Yet another school emanating from Vedanta is Shuddhadvaita, the school of a sage called Vallabhacharya who lived in the fifteenth century. This school also speaks of Lord Krishna as being the be all and end all of existence. It believes that it is bhakti alone, that is devotion to Krishna, and Krishna's grace, that finally allows a person to attain moksha.

Charvaka and Ajivika

We now come to what is referred to as the Nastika schools of Hinduism. One such is the famous Charvaka School, also known as Lokayata, which is referred to as a school of Hindu materialism. Brihaspati, traditionally, is referred to as the founder of this school. This philosophy makes it clear that the perception of the five senses is the only proper source of knowledge, while inference is conditional and may be either right or wrong. This is explained by the example of fire and smoke. Where there is smoke, the tendency may be to leap to the conclusion that it must have been caused by fire. This may not necessarily be true.

This school does not believe in karma, rebirth or an afterlife of any kind. In fact, one of the texts, the *Sarvasiddhanta Sangraha* states: 'There is no world other than this. There is no heaven and no hell. The realm of Shiva and like regions are fabricated by stupid imposters.' The text goes on to state that the enjoyment of heaven lies in eating delicious food, keeping the company of young women, using fine clothes, perfumes, garlands and sandal paste, while moksha is death, mere cessation of life breath. The wise therefore ought not to take pains to attain moksha. A fool weighs himself out by penances and fasts. Chastity and such other ordinances are laid down by clever weaklings.

The Charvakas were critical of the Vedas, stating that they suffered from errors in transmission across generations and they were often self-contradictory and tautologous. They also pointed out various contradictions of Vedic priests arguing with one another, making it clear that contradictory arguments do not hold. Specifically, they declared the Vedas to be useful as providing livelihood to priests. They held the belief that the Vedas were written by man and had no divine authority. They also went on to state that happiness trumps ethics and that while life remains, let a man live happily, let him feed on ghee even though he runs into debt.

The original works of this school, the *Brihaspati Sutras*, have been lost. We only come to know about this philosophical school of thought from commentators speaking about these texts. One such commentator makes it clear that life must be lived to the fullest; there is no life after death.

Ajivika

Another Nastika school in Hindu philosophy is the Ajivika School of thought, which is said to have been founded by Makkhali Gosala some time in the fifth century BCE. Gosala is said to have been a follower and contemporary of the

Jain Mahavira. After being disenchanted with Mahavira, he founded the Ajivika doctrine that was grounded in fatalism, known as Niyati. According to him, the predetermined fate of all living beings is the impossibility of attaining moksha or release from the endless cycle of birth, death and rebirth.

Like the Charvaka School, the Ajivikas were atheists, meaning that they did not believe in any Creator God. They also considered the karma doctrine as a fallacy because nothing depended on one's own deeds. Everything was predetermined. Ajivika metaphysics included a theory of atoms by which atoms, being eternal, join together to form living beings. This philosophy denies that there is any reward or punishment for good or bad deeds as all persons are powerless to change their fate, suffering being predestined.

Matter, pleasure, pain, the soul, the eternal do not interact to produce results which depend on free will. Ajivika belief can be summarized as follows: Life and the Universe is like a ball of pre-wrapped string which unrolls until it is done and then goes no further. The fact that Ajivikas did not believe in free will did not mean that they were pessimistic. It is important, therefore, to realize that everything is preordained and to live within this philosophy as happily as possible. Like Charvakas, the Ajivikas' original texts are lost. Whatever can be gleaned about them is solely from Buddhist works and later commentaries.

Hinduism as Practised

Hinduism as practised is essentially a positive, life affirming faith. Each Hindu is to lead life in accordance with three principles: dharma, or the practice of one's religious faith; artha or the accumulation of wealth; and kama, the pursuit of pleasure. Hinduism as practised propitiates three gods: Brahma, the Creator; Vishnu, the Preserver; and Shiva, the Destroyer. In the Puranas, the attributes of these three gods do not have such neat distinctions. Brahma is referred to as the Creator within this *trimurti*. He is depicted as a bearded man with four heads representing the four Vedas and pointing to the four directions. He is usually seated on a lotus and his mount is a swan. Since Brahma created his children from his mind, they are referred to as *manasaputra*. His consort is Goddess Saraswati, who is the embodiment of learning.

Surprisingly, Brahma does not have many temples dedicated to him because he was cursed. There are different versions of this curse. From the Shiva Purana, we get to know that Brahma and Vishnu argued as to who was the greater of the two. Shiva set up a pillar of fire and asked Brahma to go up and tell him as to where he saw the end of that fire. Shiva did the same with Vishnu, only that Vishnu would go down and tell Shiva as to where the fire ended. Brahma went up in the form of a swan and came down and lied to Shiva, saying that he did see the end of the fire. As compared to this, Vishnu went down in the form of a wild boar and came up and truthfully answered that there was no end. As a result of this, Brahma was cursed, and the curse was that he would not be worshipped by human beings.

In the Padma Purana, Brahma saw a demon, Vajranabha, trying to kill his children. He slew the demon with his weapon, the lotus flower, and in the process, lotus petals fell on the ground at three places, creating three lakes at Pushkar, in Rajasthan. Brahma then decided to perform a fire sacrifice at the Pushkar lake. Since his wife could not be present at the *yajna*, or fire sacrifice, Brahma married a young Gujjar girl, Gayatri, and completed the yajna with his new wife sitting beside him. When Saraswati finally arrived she found this young girl sitting next to Brahma, which was her rightful place, and in her anger, she cursed her husband saying that he will not be worshipped by anybody. She then relented, but only partially, saying that he could only be worshipped at Pushkar, which is why the main Brahma temple in the whole of India is only at Pushkar.

A third version of why Brahma is not worshipped outside Pushkar has reference to a sage called Bhrigu. When Bhrigu went to visit Brahma and his wife Saraswati, they were so engrossed together in music that they failed to welcome him. As a result, Bhrigu cursed Brahma stating that nobody will worship him. But he later mitigated the curse by stating that Pushkar was the only place where Brahma would be worshipped.

We come now to the second God of Hinduism, Vishnu. Vishnu is usually depicted sitting under the hood of a cobra. He has descended to Earth in the form of ten avatars or incarnations. The first avatar is the Matsya avatar or the fish avatar. We are told that an early king, Manu, finds a little fish in the palm of his hand when he performs a prayer to the waters. The fish asks Manu for a home. Manu tries to find a home for it but the fish keeps expanding and teaches Manu a lesson: that the fish itself can and does become much bigger than Manu. As a result of this, Manu realizes that his wealth cannot avail him a space large enough for the fish. When he releases this huge fish into the ocean, he realizes that it is the God Vishnu. Vishnu informs Manu of the coming destruction of the world by means of a great flood and directs Manu to collect all the creatures of the world and keep them safe on a vessel that is built by the gods. When the deluge finally occurs, Vishnu appears as a great fish with a horn to which Manu ties a rope and which, as a result of the fish shoring up the vessel on its back, keeps it in safety until the floodwaters go down. Creation is saved as a result.

In his second avatar, Vishnu arrives as Kurma, the tortoise. The devas and their enemies, the asuras, were churning an ocean of milk in order to obtain amrit or the nectar of immortality. They used the mountain Mandara as a churner, but it started to sink. Vishnu took this form in order to bear the weight of the mountain so that the devas and asuras could complete their task.

In his third incarnation, Varaha, that is the boar avatar, the gatekeepers of Vishnu's heaven, Vaikuntha, are cursed by four persons when they're stopped from seeing Vishnu. The result is that out of their hatred for Vishnu, two of them are reborn as asuras or demons who are brothers: Hiranyaksha and Hiranyakashipu. Since these brothers wrought great destruction on Earth, Vishnu came down in the form of Varaha to defeat one of the brothers, Hiranyaksha, who had abducted the Earth and carried it to the bottom of the ocean. The battle between Varaha and Hiranyaksha is believed to have lasted for a thousand years. It is only after defeating and killing Hiranyaksha that Varaha finally carried the Earth out of the ocean between its tusks and restored it.

Since the demon Hiranyakashipu still lived, the Bhagavata Purana tells us that he undertook many years of penance finally asking the Creator, Brahma, to give him a boon. The boon granted was that the demon would not die, within or outside any place, during the day or at night, nor on the ground or in the sky. Also, his death could not be brought about by any weapon, human being or animal. He could not meet death from any person living or non-living, created by Brahma or by any demi-god or demon from any of the worlds. Armed with this boon, Hiranyakashipu began to persecute those who were devotees of Vishnu. His own son, Prahlad, who had become a devotee of Vishnu, was sought to be killed by his father, but was protected by Vishnu. It is because of this boon that Vishnu had to be incarnated in the form of Narasimha or a man/ lion. Since Narasimha was neither a human being, nor a god or an animal; being part man part animal, it was possible for him to kill Hiranyakashipu. Since the other parts of the boon had also to be overcome, Narasimha attacked Hiranyakashipu at twilight when it was neither day nor night, on the threshold of a courtyard which was neither inside or outside a house, and put the demon on his thigh which was neither on Earth nor in space. Using his fingernails as weapons, he ultimately disemboweled and killed the demon.

The grandson of Prahlad, Bali, was able, with penance, to defeat Indra, the king of the gods. As he had done this, he grew arrogant and humbled all the gods and extended his rule over all the three worlds. The gods went to Vishnu to urge him to save them. During a huge fire sacrifice of King Bali, Vishnu approached the king in the form of *vamana* or a dwarf. Bali was made to promise vamana that he would grant him whatever he asked for. Vamana only asked for three pieces of land. When Bali agreed, the dwarf turned into a giant. With his first stride, he covered the earth; with the second, he covered the heavens; and finally, with the third stride, the netherworld. Bali realized that this dwarf was none other than Vishnu incarnate. As a result, the king, in humility, offered his head as a place for vamana to place his foot. Vamana did so and then granted Bali immortality, making him the ruler of *patala* or the netherworld. He also granted Bali a boon whereby he could return to Earth every year. The spring festival of Onam in Kerala is celebrated as the annual homecoming of Bali.

In his sixth incarnation, Vishnu appeared as Parashuram or Rama with an axe. He was the son of a sage called Jamadagni and his consort, Renuka. It is interesting that the axe was granted to Parashuram because it was Vishnu in the form of Parashurama who did penance to Shiva, who then granted him the axe. A king, Kartavirya Arjun, and his entourage, halted at the ashram of Jamadagni. The sage was able to feed them with the aid of a divine cow called Kamadhenu. When the king, seeing this, demanded the cow itself, Jamadagni refused. The king then took the cow by force, destroyed the ashram and left along with the cow. Parashuram, Jamadagni's son, then went to the king's palace and killed the king and destroyed his army. In revenge, the king's sons then went and killed Jamadagni. Enraged, Parashurama took a vow to kill every single Kshatriya on Earth, resulting in rivers of blood, which ultimately filled five lakes. It was only when his grandfather, the rishi Richika, appeared before him to make him halt, that he stopped this mass murder. He is believed to be immortal and is credited with creating the coastal belt of Karnataka and Kerala by throwing his axe in the sea, displacing water and creating the first reclaimed land in known history.

In his next avatar, Vishnu came down to Earth as Rama, the king of Ayodhya. The story of Rama is narrated in one of the greatest epics of all time, the Ramayana. While in exile from his own kingdom with his wife Sita and his brother Lakshman, Sita got abducted by Ravana, the ten-headed king of Lanka. Rama went with his army to Lanka, killed Ravana and brought back Sita. After they returned to Ayodhya, they were crowned as king and queen and ruled over Ayodhya in what was celebrated as Rama Rajya or ideal rule. The festival of Diwali in India is celebrated to commemorate Rama's defeat of King Ravana of Lanka, and his eventual return to Ayodhya.

In his eighth avatar, Vishnu came to Earth as Lord Krishna. Krishna was the eighth son of Vasudev and Devaki, and was born to slay his tyrannical uncle, Kamsa. Being divine, he proclaimed his message to mankind through the Bhagavad Gita, which we have already referred to in some detail. Lord Krishna sided with the five Pandavas in the fratricidal Kurukshetra war which is referred to in great detail in what can arguably be called the greatest epic ever written, the Mahabharata. It is Krishna as Arjun's charioteer who steers the Pandavas to victory over their cousins. Krishna is widely worshipped all over India, him being the central character not only in the Mahabharata, but also in the Bhagavat Purana.

In his ninth avatar, Vishnu is said to have come to Earth as the Buddha.

The tenth and final form of Vishnu, Kalki, will come as a saviour at the end of the Kali Yuga.

He will be riding a white horse, and his sword will be drawn and blazing like a comet. He will come at the end of time when evil and persecution will prevail and dharma will have vanished, to begin yet another cycle of existence in the Satya Yuga.

It is interesting to note that the ten incarnations of Vishnu follow Darwin's theory of evolution. Matsya, the first incarnation of Vishnu, is in the form of a fish; according to the theory of evolution, life first began under water. Kurma, the tortoise, is an amphibian who lives both in the water and on land. Varaha, the wild boar, has reference to early animal life. Vamana, the dwarf, is the first human incarnation of Vishnu, referring to ancient man. Thereafter, Vishnu appears as a human being throughout. It is only the avatar Narasimha who is out of line with evolutionary theory, as Vishnu comes down as half-man half-lion for the specific purpose of killing a demon Hiranyakashipu, who he could not kill unless he came to Earth in this form.

We now come to the third great God in Hinduism, Shiva. Just as Brahma creates and Vishnu maintains or preserves, Shiva destroys or transforms. He's often depicted with a moon on his forehead, and with a third eye with which he burns desire to ashes.. This gives rise to the theory that his origin is really in the Vedic God, Rudra. His body is covered with ashes, reminding human beings that to death we shall return and that it is the pursuit of the eternal self alone that can escape this. His hair is matted and his throat is blue. This is because he drank poison that was churned up from the ocean in order to save mankind from being poisoned. His wife Parvati squeezed his neck, stopping the poison in his neck so as to save the rest of his body. It is for this reason that the neck alone is blue as a result of the poison being there. The Ganges River made her abode in Shiva's head, and Shiva is often shown garlanded with a serpent. Typically, he carries a trident called the *trishul* which represents the three gunas: sattva, rajas and tamas. A small drum is also placed in his hand when he becomes the famous dancer Nataraja. Nandi, a bull, serves as Shiva's mount. His abode is in Mount Kailash in the Himalayas, he being the only God who lives on Earth. His consort is Goddess Parvati, who assumes many forms including a warrior goddess who is worshipped as Durga.

The Puranas tell us the story of Daksha, whom we encounter in mandala 10, chapter 72, of the Rigveda, having a daughter called Sati who gets married to Shiva. Father-in-law and son-in-law clash as a result of which Daksha does not invite Shiva to his yajna or fire sacrifice. As this is insulting to Shiva, Sati comes to her father's yajna on her own and becomes the first sati in history, that is the first woman to immolate herself, at the ceremony to protest against her husband's exclusion. This so shocks Shiva that he retires to the mountains in meditation and austerity. Sati then gets reborn as Parvati.

Parvati, in turn, is spoken of as an ideal wife and mother and gives birth to two sons, Ganesh and Kartikeya. Ganesh is the famous God worshipped in Maharashtra and south India who has an elephant's head on a human body. The reason why there is an elephant's head is explained in an interesting story. Parvati wanted to bathe and be protected while bathing, as a result of which she created a boy out of turmeric paste and infused life into it, thus giving birth to Ganesh. Parvati ordered Ganesh not to allow anybody to enter. After a while, Shiva returned home and tried to enter the house but was stopped by Ganesh. Shiva, infuriated, lost his temper and severed the boy's head. When Parvati came out and saw her dead son, she demanded that Shiva restore Ganesh to life at once. This Shiva did by taking another life, as he promised her that he would take the life of the first person that he saw in order to bring Ganesh back to life. He saw an elephant, so he cut off its head and placed it on Ganesh's lifeless body so that Ganesh could come back to life.

Interestingly enough, Ganesh also has one tusk, the other tusk being broken. One reason given is that a single tusk is used to reach God, so that all forms of dualism are then overcome. There are other interesting reasons as to why Ganesh's tusk was broken. When Sage Vyas began writing the Mahabharata epic, he turned to Ganesh to write down whatever he dictated. Ganesh agreed only on the condition that Vyas recite the poem uninterrupted, without pause. Vyas, in turn, told Ganesh that he could not write until he understood everything that he heard. This being the modus operandi agreed upon, once the dictation began, Ganesh's pen broke, but he had to continue writing and the only way he could do so was to break off his tusk and use it as a pen. Another interesting story about how Ganesh lost his tusk is when Parashuram, the avatar of Vishnu, went to pay a visit to Ganesh's father, Shiva. Ganesh blocked Parashuram's way, thereby incurring his wrath. Parshuram then hurled his axe at Ganesh, who lost his tusk as a result.

Kartikeya is also largely worshipped in south India and is called by many names, one of them being Murugan. Many festivals are celebrated as a result of the worship of Kartikeya. One of them is Thaipusam, which is celebrated on the full moon day in the Tamil month of Thai. Another is Panguni Uthiram which occurs on the full moon night of the month of Panguni. Karthika Deepam is a south Indian festival of lights. Kanda Sashti, which falls in the month of Aippasi, is where Kartikeya commemorates his victory as Murugan over the demon Soorapadman.

We now come to the *yuga* cycles in Hinduism. Each yuga cycle consists of four yugas or ages: Krita or Satya, Treta, Dvapara and Kali, consisting of 43,20,000 years of 12,00,000 divine years. There are 71 such cycles in one maha yuga and 1000 such cycles in one *kalpa,* which is a single day of Brahma. Through each of the yugas, humanity's general moral and physical state declines, and in Kali Yuga it is supposed to become the most debased. Satya Yuga is supposed to consist of 4800 divine years as against the Treta Yuga which consists of 3600 such years; Dvapara Yuga consists of 2400 years, and finally, Kali Yuga consists of 1200 such years. Time is, therefore, cyclical and not linear, with each cycle ending in hope, as when in cyclical time, it is darkest at five in the morning, when dawn cannot be far away.

PART IV

Reincarnation: Its Nuances and Pitfalls

Introduction

Six great philosophers permeated the fourth and fifth centuries BCE. Two were in Greece, two in India and two in China. Pythagoras of Samos lived between 570 to 495 BCE. He created the Pythagorean theorem in geometry that states that the square of two sides of a right-angled triangle is equal to the square of the hypotenuse of the said triangle. Pythagoras was a vegetarian. Once, he saw the soul of a friend trapped in the body of a little puppy which was being beaten. 'Do not beat it,' he said. He had no doubt that human beings can reincarnate and can also transmigrate to becoming animals. He believed that in the circle of existence, such reincarnation and transmigration is eternal.

The great philosopher Plato followed Pythagoras in this, although long after him: between 424 and 348 BCE.

In the last chapter of the book *Republic*, Er, a warrior, has a near-death experience and comes back into his inert body after twelve days. Just like Arda Viraf, a priest who lived in Sasanian Persia, in 230 CE. He narrates that he had visited heaven, hell and purgatory. These are all temporary in nature, as the soul reincarnates after the time spent in these places. The choice of the next incarnation depends on how one has spent one's past life.

A person may wish to have power in the next life, not realizing that he may be born as a dictator who then murders his own children and goes to hell as a result. In the book *Phaedo*, reincarnation and transmigration are both spoken about as punishments for the evil done in past lives. In the *Phaedo*, the only way of deliverance is to get out of this cycle.

Both Confucius and Lao Tzu lived in the same period, in China, but said nothing on reincarnation. They emphasized life and not the afterlife, with different philosophies of their own. According to Confucius, the worship of ancestors and the living of a life of virtue is how a person must lead his life. According to Lao Tzu, what is important is that in blending with nature, one does something wise, for it is not possible to fight with nature. True happiness consists in being passive; nature shows us that flowing water can round the edges of hard material like rock. The ancient Shinto religion, practised in Japan, does not mention reincarnation, neither does the ancient Egyptian religion.

When it comes to the theistic religion Zoroastrianism, which is the oldest of the monotheistic faiths, there is no mention of reincarnation. This, however, comes with a caveat. In chapter 29 of the *Yajashne*, in a conference that occurs between God and the archangels in heaven, Zarathushtra, even before he is born on Earth, is stated to be a person who is fit to come to Earth as a saviour/redeemer.

In Judaism, the Prophet Jeremaiah is also spoken of before he is born, who, like Zarathushtra, will come to Earth as a prophet in troubled times. Even though the Old Testament does not explicitly refer to reincarnation, yet the *Kabala* or mystical text of the Jews explicitly refers to the many past lives that humans live here on Earth.

Similarly, Christianity, in the person of Jesus Christ, does not specifically refer to reincarnation. Except that, in answer to some of his critics, when Jesus spoke of the earlier Jewish prophets, he said, 'Even before them I am'. Also, in the gospel of St John, he is referred to as the word who co-existed in eternity with God. John the Baptist is said to be the Prophet Elijah, who returns to Earth as John. Of the Church fathers, it is only Origen who believed in reincarnation. But the Council of Constantinople, held in 553 CE, is itself not clear on whether the teachings of Origen are anathematized. However, the Third Council of Constantinople held in 680 CE, gave its assent to five previous synods in one of which the teachings of Origen were anathematized. Likewise, the Quran does not speak of reincarnation.

Jainism

Jainism flourished in the Indo-Gangetic plain even before the Aryans settled in north India. Jainism was preached by twenty-three tirthankaras before Mahavir was born in the sixth century BCE. It is important to remember that Jainism is an atheistic religion—it gives reasons as to why God does not exist. Wholly compatible with an atheistic religion is the absence of a divine plan, and hence the wheel of reincarnation which is endless and meaningless. Time is cyclical, ascending and descending. It may take many million lives to reach human existence which may, in one lifetime, depending on one's karma, require the person to be reborn as an ant or something other, and carry on in this endless cycle of death and rebirth. Consequently, nirvana in Jainism is returning to the jiva's pure joy and immortality, unsullied by *pudgal*, or matter.

There are six dravyas, or substances, that are said to be eternal. Five of them are ajiva, i.e., not animate. They are: (i) pudgal, or matter; (ii) dharma, or medium of motion; for e.g., water in which fish move; (iii) adharma, or medium of rest; (iv) *akash*, or space; (v) *kaal*, or time.

Jiva is a soul which is uncreated, eternal, and of an infinite number in the Universe. Each soul is endowed with *chetana*, i.e., consciousness, and *upyoga*, i.e, perception. All human and other living beings have souls which are in the shape and size of the physical body they inhabit. There is no universal soul of brahman in Jainism. Though eternal, the six dravyas are constantly subject to change, which is contrary to Hindu and Buddhist thought, as something eternal cannot be subjected to change. According to the Jains, the clay which makes the pot is eternal; the pot may break and therefore die.

Jainism believes that a soul may pass through eighty-four lakh lives to be born as a human being, depending on four different types of karmas. The first is Namakarma, which is divided into ninety-eight parts of the future body. The second is the Gotrakarma, where birth takes place, which predicts the spirituality of the future incarnation. The third is the Vedniyakarma, which predicts future happiness, and the fourth is the Ayuhkarma, which predicts length of life. Sallekhana, the starving to death of an old Jain is said to be best for rebirth in a happy or good state, as the soul then rapidly develops spiritually.

Jainism has the maximum range of incarnations as it believes that one may transmigrate from being an inanimate object such as a water body all the way through plant and animal existence, then human existence and finally the existence of the gods.

One other important thing in Jain thought is that there is no intermediate state between death and rebirth. What is reincarnated, namely, the soul, moves into a new physical body immediately after death. What is also important to remember is that, this being the case, the *shraadh* ritual of the Hindus where the children of the dead person look after such a person in the intermediate state by ritual offerings and chanting of prayers until such person is reborn, is rejected.

In Jainism there is no belief in God; karma is inexorable, there being nothing such as the deity's grace in one's spiritual development.

Buddhism

As is well known, Buddhism rejects extreme views and follows what it called the middle path. It expressly rejects the teachings of Jainism as well as Gosala, who founded the Ajivika sect. According to Gosala, everything is fated to happen, and nothing is left to free will.

In Buddhism, what is important is that karma is the aggregate of good and bad deeds. A differentiation is made between past karma, which is acts done which have already reaped their reward, and acts that accumulate, which depend in turn upon four things: (1) intent, (2) whether the act is completed, (3) whether there are regrets or counter actions, and (4) the reaping of a reward yet to be given.

Buddhism does not believe in reincarnation of a soul. In fact, the Buddha preached the doctrine of *anatta* which means that no soul exists. Thus, according to Mahayana Buddhism, what reincarnates into another being is one of the five skandas, namely, consciousness, whereas according to Theravada Buddhism, genetics and character get reincarnated into another being (the two other skandas being feeling and perception).

Buddhism has a range of transmigration which begins from living substances such as algae all the way to the gods in the heavens and to demonic worlds.

In Buddhism, according to the *Tibetan Book of the Dead*, consciousness of a dead person is in the intermediate bardo state, which usually lasts for a period of over a month before the law of karma finds the next being into which the dead person's consciousness reincarnates.

Hinduism

Vedic Hinduism

A reading of the Rigveda will show that though there is a developed concept of heaven, there is no developed concept of reincarnation or hell. The only dissenting voice is of the former Indian President Radhakrishnan, who found reincarnation in some abstruse verses of the Rigveda.

Hell in the Rigveda is at best an underground darkness, something like sheol in Judaism, in which a dead person exists for all eternity. The people of the Rigveda loved life and feared death. The first man to travel to a heavenly abode after death was King Yama. Fierce dogs guard the entrance to heaven. The dove and the owl are considered messengers of death. When the soul leaves the body and enters the heavenly realms, it is accompanied by Agni (the Fire God), and Savitr and Pusan (solar deities). The first heaven is the abode of King Yama which is called the heaven of the moon. This is where persons who make sacrifices to the gods, and philanthropists, go. The second heaven is the heaven of the Sun, that of Savitr and Surya (solar deities). This is where people of exceptional merit go. The third and highest form of heaven is the heaven of Vishnu, in which seers devoted to the gods ultimately go. Once in heaven, all bodily imperfections and sicknesses dissipate. Heaven is described as the land of milk and honey, where there is eternal light, and where songs are heard. (Rigveda, chapter 135.7) There is nobody who is weak or strong; all are equal. In the Atharvaveda, it is also an abode in which there are sexual pleasures (Book IV, chapter 34.2).

In the Rigveda, as mentioned earlier, Daksha produces Aditi and Aditi produces Daksha. Aditi eats rice after offering the same to the gods as a result of which she produces eight *adityas* (solar deities). It is only when she ate all the rice herself without offering any rice to the gods that she produced *Mart Anda,* the dead egg, which is mankind, who alone of her children, is slated to die.

Upanishads

At the end of the Vedas came the Upanishads of which the Brihadaranayka, Chandogya and Kaushitaki all speak of reincarnation. These ideas are also reflected in the Puranas, more particularly the Garudapurana. In the Chandogya (Book V, chapters 4–10) and Brihadaranayka Upanishads (Book VI, chapter 2, verse 9–16), what is described after a soul leaves the body is that it either enters the realms of *pitriyan* or *devayan*. Associated with the realm of pitriyan is the doctrine of five fires in which the soul exhausts the merit it has earned on Earth in five transitory stations: heaven, ether, Earth, man and woman. Such a soul is, after exhaustion of its virtues, reborn, depending on the merit earned—as a Brahmin, Kshatriya or Vaishya or, if demerits outweigh merits, as a dog, hog or an outcast. On the other hand, according to the doctrine of the two ways, by going to devayan, the soul goes upwards through various realms of light, then lightning, and then to brahman in which it experiences through chitta, that is consciousness, ananda, that is eternal bliss.

According to the Vedas, which includes the Upanishads, (being Vedanta) and the Dharmasutras—which are commentaries on the Upanishads—a person's immortality is in the creation of progeny (see the Apastamba Dharmasutra). In fact, death rituals in Hinduism create, every day, some part of the future body, for a period of ten days after death. *Pinda* is a ball of rice which is mixed with seed and milk which is meant to be food for the dead soul, in the transition between death and rebirth.

Puranas and Brahmanas

In the Puranas, the Garudapurana, the Agnipurana and the Brahamapurana, in particular, speak of reincarnation.

The Puranas go back to the fifth century CE, and are eighteen in number. They are divided into groups of six, each belonging either to Brahma, Vishnu or Shiva. The Garudapuran belongs to the Vishnu group of Puranas. Garuda, the bird, narrates what he sees to Sage Kashyapa, his father, who in turn narrates it to Sage Vyasa, who in turn narrates it to Lord Shiva. It is stated that when a person dies, the evil that he does is exhausted in hell after which he can then be born as an animal, plant, insect, human being who is diseased, a low-caste person or a human being born with physical deformities. A person who discards his wife wrongly is born as an animal, who is then killed by a hunter. Likewise, a person who does good exhausts the good done in the previous life in heaven, and is then reborn in the house of kings or of nobles of good character. Rebirth can take place in the form of a seed, an egg, an embryo or through sweat. After death, an aerial body is formed within ten days, provided the necessary ceremonies are performed by the next of kin. This body gets eaten up on the eleventh and twelfth day and is replaced by a temporary body on the thirteenth day, which then goes to the abode of Yama for a period of one year. The story is told of Sudev, the Vaishya, who had nobody to perform his death ceremony, as a result of which he wandered around the Earth as a ghost. Fate is described quite simply as accumulated merit or sin of past lives. When conceived, the soul recollects its past lives when in the womb, but when it is born, maya causes it to be confused and deluded, as a result of which it forgets its past lives.

The gross physical body becomes a subtle astral body as big as a thumb within twelve days of death. Pinda offerings by descendants on Earth keep this body going, which then becomes a *preta* body or temporary body. After one year of hovering around in suspended animation, the preta body becomes an 'experience' body. This experience body may reap good or evil, depending upon past karma. This body then experiences bliss in heaven or torment in hell, until all its karmas get exhausted, at which point the soul comes back either in a human form from heaven or in an animal form from hell. This Purana also speaks of a child being born with whatever his father has in his mind at the time of impregnation of its mother. The Padmapurana says the same thing but the time is shifted to the time of death of the father.

Shankaracharya states that like a caterpillar, one casts out one's previous form and *apurva* (karmic merit) then takes the soul to heaven after which, when one's merit is over, transmigration takes place by the soul's karmic residue, *anusuya*. The Markandeyapurana states that every soul goes upwards from an ant to a human being in the worst form 'like a hunchback', then through each of the four varnas, and finally goes to the heaven of the gods or vice versa, depending on the karma accumulated.

However, in the Puranas, we get the idea of remedial action which can be taken in this life to swim against the tide of karma. The Garudapuran in the Dhanvantari Samhita speaks of the wheel of existence or the sansar chakra. According to the Linga and Shiva Purana, meditation and renunciation are antidotes by which the tide of karma can be stemmed. Karma can also be conquered by bhakti or devotion to God, which can make the Almighty's grace deliver a person from sin. Also, a wife's chastity can release her husband from sin.

In the Matsyapurana, bathing at a shrine removes bad karma. Gods are free from the doctrine of karma. So far as human beings are concerned, karma consists of three things: (1) Fate, or what is done to man, (2) man's own actions, and (3) time, that is the past, the present and the future.

The Mahabharata elaborates on this, stating that karma can be (1) providential acts of God, (2) divine ordinance, (3) fate which is equal to past karma, (4) time, (5) death, (6) nature, and (7) human action. In fact, the Mahabharata, in Book III, speaks of Sage Markandeya speaking to Yudhishthira. According to the sage, at one time, all persons were fully pure and used to migrate between heaven and Earth. However, lust and wrath have made human beings fall and become animals, demons, etc. Rebirth after death takes place instantly like a shadow following its physical body.

In the Puranas, one very important aspect of the karma theory is the transference of merit or demerit both to and from parents and children. Thus, the dead father can get, by way of transfer, good karma from those who are living, through the pinda, so that in an astral body he may rise to heaven. Equally, a dying father may bequeath some of his good karma to his children just before his death. Transference also occurs through sexual contact between husband and wife. However, in the Mahabharata, there can be no transfer of karma.

King Somaka had a son called Jantu. A Brahmin priest told him to sacrifice his child if he wanted many more sons. On the king's behalf, the priest did so, as a result of which a hundred wives of the king gave birth to a hundred sons. Jantu was reborn as the eldest son. For the murder of Jantu, the Brahmin goes straight to hell. When the king is told this, he says that it was at his request that the priest carried out the killing of the first Jantu, and that he should therefore really be the one going to hell. Lord Dharma says that cannot happen as there can be no karmic transfer. Nobody experiences the fruits of another's action.

Another interesting story in the Mahabharata (Book I, 104) is when Sage Brihaspati rapes his pregnant sister-in-law. The embryo within kicks Brihaspati's semen out. The sage curses the embryo, which is then born blind as Dirghatamas, the blind sage.

The law of karma

Karma can broadly be divided into two types, namely, active and passive. In Hinduism, passive karma predominates, that is, what is done to you in this life is dependent upon past accumulated karmas in previous lives. One example is a Brahmin boy born as a leper because in his past life he had been a murderer. In Buddhism, on the other hand, emphasis is on what is called active karma, which is that what you have done in your past lives accumulates as bad karma to make you do evil deeds to others in this life.

The law of active and passive karma turns the law of pre-destination on its head. Active and passive karma account for free will alone, which then leads to current and future living conditions.

In Zoroastrianism what is predetermined is one's birth, wife, children, power and property. However, ones onward journey in life, which is going to heaven or hell, depends on each individual's ethical behaviour on earth.

On nature depends eating, walking, sleeping and toilet.

On character depends friendship, goodness, generosity and rectitude.

On heredity depends intellect, understanding, body, stature and appearance.

In Hinduism, there are four different kinds of destiny, depending on one's karma: (1) Hedonism and self-indulgence gives only treasures in this world but not in the next; (2) Asceticism in this world by those who are selfless leads to them reaping the reward of the next world but not this one; (3) Human beings who live by dharma, artha and kama will get the pleasures of both worlds; and (4) Those who are ignorant and immoral will reap the reward of a wretched existence in both worlds.

In the Charaka Samhita, which is a medical treatise, disease can be caused by karma from a previous life. One's fate is dependent upon one's past karma. Atreya says that one's life span depends on how one lives life. The axle of a wheel is given as an example. This axle will function till it wears out. It wears out early if there is an excessive load on the wagon; or if there are bad roads; or if there are clumsy drivers. Disease can be brought on not only by karma, but also the wrath of the gods, and by bad living, that is living by cultivating bad habits.

Plus points of the theory of reincarnation

1. The greatest plus point of reincarnation is that it explains why persons suffer—why a person is born lame or dumb or why a person is dogged with misfortune.

2. Since the law of karma mandates that a person will reap what he sows, it leads persons to behave in accordance with moral constraints.

3. Since transmigration is part and parcel of the theory, it teaches human beings to be compassionate to all other living beings.

4. It explains child prodigies. Mozart must have been a master musician in his past life to be able to compose music as a child of five.

Objections to the theory of reincarnation

1. If the idea of the karma theory is to punish a person for what he has done in his previous life, the person who is being punished does not know what he is being punished for as there is no memory of any past life (we have the disingenuous explanation of the embryo remembering its past lives until it is in the womb. At birth, maya [illusion] makes its forget them [*Garudapurana*]). Consequently, the soul cannot remember its past lives so as to correct itself in its present incarnation.

2. Reincarnation is ostrich-like. There are billions of planets which may have other forms of life to which a soul may be born; it does not have to come back to Earth. I am reminded of a cartoon strip called 'Lurie's opinion' in the magazine *Newsweek* which showed the Viking spacecraft land on planet Mars with one rock facing another, in which the first rock

tells the second rock, 'Don't move, they might take us for rocks.'

3. Transmigration involves human souls being reborn as plants and animals. There are many more plants and animals than there have been human beings on Earth. Do these plants and animals which have not transmigrated from human beings have souls, and do these souls reincarnate among themselves?

4. Unlike humans, plants and animals have no moral ladder to climb up and down. How then do they have any doctrine of karma which applies to them? A tiger survives by killing other animals for food. In doing so, it lives in accordance with its nature and does not transgress any moral law. As a matter of fact, it often dies because of starvation, a Jain death, as being a solitary animal, it cannot hunt because of old age or sickness.

5. The assumption on which karma and transmigration are based is that being reborn as an animal or a plant is a punishment; most animals and plants live happily in nature. Furthermore, no differentiation is made between animals and plants who suffer and those who don't. For example, a dog may be chained and beaten throughout its life and may be miserable. Another dog may be born in a dog lover's home and be cared for better than a human being.

6. There is also an internal contradiction as it is assumed that to be born as a human is better than

being born as an animal or plant. But, as a human, one may be born deformed or may suffer throughout life, making human existence more miserable than animal or plant life. Also, a person's mental state is completely ignored; some deformed person may be happy, another sad.

7. The theory of reincarnation flies in the face of the law of heredity. How does one inherit one's parents characteristics if one has come loaded with one's own past karma?

8. In reincarnation, what is reborn is not clear. Is it an eternal soul, is it consciousness, is it nature and heredity, is it the mind as we know it?

9. Reincarnation has no justice built into the law, which is inexorable: an eye for an eye and a tooth for a tooth.

10. The Church Father Tertullian had two objections to reincarnation on the ground that humans reincarnate only into humans.

   a. People die at different ages, yet are all reborn as infants. There is no continuity of past lives; and

   b. If all souls have to reincarnate, how is the human population not the same, but growing by leaps and bounds.

11. The theory is inconsistent with evolution—evolution is consistent with there being a God as there is constant improvement—time is linear, not cyclical. Also, an ape becomes a human and not vice versa.

No other plant or animal species becomes human. Whereas reincarnation is consistent with atheism as there is no divine plan but only a game of snakes and ladders. One may become human after many plant and animal lives, and slip back into such lives, moving slowly upwards all over again.

12. Karma follows a particular law—as you sow so shall you reap. A law without a law giver or enforcer is illogical, and transmigrating from man to animal or plant and vice versa reveals an extremely arbitrary law without there being any law giver or enforcer or law to be followed, as in the case of animals and plants.

13. What happens in the interregnum between death and rebirth is another problem. How does a human soul, depending on its karma, dependent on its deeds, find exactly the right womb in which to be born, and which agency sees that this is matched correctly? In short, for an evil person, how does punishment (rebirth) fit the crime (birth)?

14. Reincarnation cannot explain Alzheimer patients. A person who has Alzheimer's has a brain that has been attacked by the disease. This brings out in bold relief, the difference between the physical brain, what is called the mind, and what is called the soul. Since Alzheimer's is attributable to a deterioration of the physical brain which is reflected in the mind of the human being, is the soul something different from the mind so as to be completely separate and distinct

and be born as such? And if this is so, then how does the doctrine of karma work?

15. Seance, or the art of communicating with spirits in another world, shows that spirits who may have died on Earth hundreds of years ago, do not come back to Earth but continue to live in another plane of existence. On the other hand, we have books of persons like Ian Stevenson, who speaks of persons remembering their previous lives. Of course, Paul Edwards has refuted such instances in a book entitled *Reincarnation: A Critical Examination.*

PART V

Suffering

Suffering is a human condition which needs explanation. If proper answers can be given as to the cause of suffering and the way out of suffering, that will itself be justification enough for the writing of this book. How each of the world's great religions deal with this phenomenon is a matter of great interest to any seeker after truth.

In Hinduism, on a reading of the six Hindu philosophical schools, the Upanishads and the Bhagavad Gita, the doctrine of karma leads one to believe that one's suffering is entirely caused by oneself. Suffering in the present life is the result of the accumulation of bad karma in previous lives. Another cause of suffering is the ignorance of the three paths that will ultimately lead to moksha or a deliverance from the endless cycle of reincarnation, in which the soul then experiences complete bliss, either by itself or by its merger with the larger, universal soul, brahman. The three paths that have been outlined in Hinduism are gyana yoga or the path of knowledge, bhakti yoga or the path of devotion to God, and karma yoga or the path of doing one's duty to the best of one's ability. Gyana yoga as we have seen is nothing but right knowledge which leads to the fact that one's atman or soul or self is nothing but a reflection of the universal self, brahman, and the realization of this self then leads to liberation. This is the path advocated by the schools of Samkhya, Yoga, Nyaya, Vaisheshika and advaita in Vedanta.

The second path, the path of bhakti, is a theistic path, which leads to moksha, which is the longing for the love and grace of a Creator God, who then by His grace, lifts the soul up to realms in which it experiences bliss. The third path, which is the path strongly advocated by the Bhagavad Gita, is the path of karma yoga which speaks of the doing of one's duty to the best of one's ability after which it is important to live on only what is necessary, and renounce the fruits of this work so that through performing one's duty, one can again be liberated.

When we come to the monotheistic religions, Zoroastrianism has to be dealt with in two parts. The Zoroastrianism of the Gathas or what was preached by Prophet Zarathustra makes it clear that suffering is as a result of wrong moral choice, just as its obverse, happiness, is the result of the correct moral choice by following the path of truth. In younger Zoroastrianism, that is Zoroastrianism that was preached and practised during the Sasanian period of history in Iran, the spirit that chose evil, Angra Mainyu, in the Gathas, now becomes a full blown devil who counteracts everything that a good Creator God does. Suffering, therefore, is attributed only to the acts of the devil, who afflicts mankind with everything that is bad, ranging from physical disease to mental torture. In this world view, man is said to struggle against evil or the devil in order to establish a realm of perfect happiness in which suffering will go once and for all only when the devil is finally expelled from this Earth, which an all good and omniscient God knows will happen, at the end of the appointed period of 12,000 years, after which mankind will live in the companionship of God in complete bliss and forever.

In Judaism, another monotheistic faith, God covenants with Abraham, the founder of the religion and chooses the Jews to be a model people so that the ethical way of life may be a lesson to mankind as a whole. The suffering of the Jews is as a result of the breach of this covenant, which alienates themselves from God. The Book of Job, one of the books of the Bible in the Old Testament, deals only with the aspect of suffering. Job was said to be a man who was good and upright, who feared God and didn't know evil. He was very wealthy. Satan, a fallen angel, makes his first appearance in the Bible in this book, and says to God that it is time now to test Job and to see whether Job will love God in the same fashion even after misfortunes are heaped on him. God permitted Satan to so test Job by the latter inflicting misfortunes upon him. Job's oxen were stolen, his sheep and servants were destroyed by lightning, his camels were taken by Chaldeans. His house was blown down and his children killed in a hurricane. Despite these terrible calamities, Job continued to love God in the same way by saying, 'The Lord gave and the Lord has taken away. Blessed be the name of the Lord.'

After Satan's first attempt failed, he again obtained God's permission to tempt Job on the condition that he spared his life. So Satan smote Job with sore boils all over his body. At this point, Job's wife gave in and told him, 'You still retain your integrity. Curse God and die!' But Job rebuked her saying she spoke as a foolish woman. At this point, three of Job's friends, hearing of his condition, came to mourn with him and to comfort him. Job, given his affliction, cursed the day he was born, and gave his friends the opportunity to tell him that this affliction must be the result of previous sin. They kept on telling him that he should submit himself to the justice of God. Job acknowledged God's omnipotence and wisdom but questioned his justice. He turned from his friends' insinuations against an all-good God to a direct challenge to God saying, 'My desire is that the Almighty would answer in my affliction.' At this point of the narrative, a young man called Elihu intervened and criticized Job and his friends, telling them that God sent affliction only to prove or to purge the sufferer and urged Job not to question God, because God is great and we know Him not.

At last God spoke to Job out of a whirlwind. He did not make any reference to Job's affliction and asked Job, 'Who am I and who are you?' In a series of portrayals, God displayed the world of nature in all its glory and magnificence, thus changing Job's bitterness to wonder and awe. At this point he said, 'I can now see that you can do everything and no thought can be withheld from you. I have not only heard you but I have now seen you. I, therefore, abhor myself and repent in dust and ashes.' God then spoke to Job's friends, and said, 'My wrath is kindled against thee, for ye have not spoken the thing that is right as my servant Job had.'

God thereafter gave Job twice as much as he had before, so that Job lived till a 140 years, saw his sons and his sons' sons even up to four generations, being old and full of days. The Jewish answer, therefore, to the condition of suffering is to bear with it and to continue to worship God because suffering is only to test man's love for God and to purge him from sin.

When we come to the next great monotheistic religion, Christianity, it speaks of the first man Adam and the original sin of disobedience to God which has caused mankind's suffering. However, Jesus tells us that there is hope because this Earth passes by like a flash, and it is the life that is to come that is real. In the life that is to come, suffering is completely removed, if you live in accordance with God's commandments and believe that Jesus Christ came down to Earth and suffered himself to take on mankind's sins so that God could forgive them. Jesus reminds us that earthly suffering lasts for only a moment in time. Everlasting life is mankind's lot if one lives by God's commandments.

When we come to the other great monotheistic faith, Islam, we are told to have faith and completely surrender to God's will because God only does what is good for us. Suffering ultimately reminds us of God and the fact that we should return to God. It echoes what is said in Judaism and Christianity, that suffering is also a means of testing a person, so that his faith in the Almighty becomes rock-like. Also the emphasis is on the life to come. If one does good deeds in the name of God and believes in judgement, the first judgement takes place on an individual's death, after which he spends the rest of his days in heaven. The second judgement takes place on Judgement Day, after which all good souls will be resurrected to lead a life on Earth as immortal beings, with complete happiness and with no suffering whatsoever.

In Sikhism, another great monotheistic faith, suffering cannot be attributed at all to God who is all good. Suffering is as a result of the selfishness of a human being and it is only selfless action on Earth which benefits other human beings that pleases their Creator, so that their suffering gets alleviated. In the most recent monotheistic faith, Bahaism, the Judeo-Christian Islamic tradition is reiterated. Suffering is a mere temporary manifestation of a reminder to seek out God. Real suffering consists of the separation of the human being from God. This suffering only goes when there is a strong desire to be near to God so that God's effulgence then takes over and removes all misery.

When it comes to religions which do not have God as their central feature, we find a very different view of suffering. In Jainism, for example, you are told that you are to concentrate on the suffering of every other living being and the mortification of yourself is a means of reminding you how others suffer, as a result of which the central principle of Jainism, ahimsa or non-violence to every other living being, is what is to be practised at all times by every living Jain. Thus, Jainism deflects the suffering that each individual goes through by asking him to alleviate the suffering of others.

Buddhism has a very different view. In Buddhism, suffering is the central tenet of the faith as it is the first of the Four Noble Truths that Gautam Buddha preached in his first sermon. Buddhism concentrates on one's own suffering, but does not go into why it is there. Since it is there, do not waste time in going into useless questions as to how and why it exists but merely alleviate it. And the alleviation of one's own suffering is by the realization that it is caused by greed and desire beyond what is necessary. The best way of getting rid of such desire is following of the Middle or Noble Eightfold Path that we have spoken of earlier in this book.

Confucianism's answer to suffering is behaving like an ordinary human being and not like the Superior Man who lives by virtue, filial piety and the worship of his ancestors. It is only when you lead life in accord with Confucius's sayings that you lead life like a Superior Man and therefore, alleviate suffering in yourself and in all others.

Taoism, another faith which does not speak of any Creator God, believes in the passive benign principle which creates and governs all things, the Tao. Suffering here is obviously caused by action, as every action which is against nature will have a reaction which will cause suffering. Therefore, the best way is to live passively in accordance with nature and to let things flow by themselves. The non-interference with nature is what leads to, through various techniques of meditation and otherwise, a realization of the Tao and to bliss.

It can thus be seen that all the world religions have something significant to say about why we suffer and the way out of suffering. A lot is to be learnt from all of them.

Conclusion

H aving gone through the essence of all of the world's great religions, what do we find? Is it possible to have a neat division of metaphysical outlook? Theistic vs non-theistic? Pigeonholing any of them into logically neat divisions is difficult because within primarily theistic religions such as Hinduism, there can be vastly different clashing ideologies. Equally, the Tao, which is not exactly brahman but conceptually is something close, being the cause of everything, again does not fit into this neat pattern as there is no Creator God in Taoism. If we look at the world's religions with time in mind, that is whether they concentrate upon the past, present and the future, again we find that there is no neat division. Hinduism, that is the Rigveda, the six philosophical schools, the Upanishads and the Bhagavad Gita, definitely focus on the past as it is many past karmas and past lives that have led to one's present situation. At the same time, Hinduism also looks to the future because it is important to get out of the present, once and for all, as it is to attain moksha or liberation from rebirth.

We also find that there are both theistic and non-theistic faiths that seem to focus essentially on the present and not

on the past or the future. Thus we have seen that Judaism
has no concept of past lives except in a much later work,
the Kabbalah, and equally no developed concept of an
afterlife. The focus is on the worship of one God and living
in accordance with His commandments. Another theistic
religion, the Sikh religion, also focuses on the present, but
with an eye to the past, as reincarnation is certainly part and
parcel of the religion.

Buddhism is a faith which focuses only on the present
and speaks of reincarnation as something to be liberated
from in the future. There is no future of a soul either living
in bliss or merging with a super soul. Equally, Confucianism
and Taoism also focus on the present, teaching mankind
how to live life without any focus on what has gone past
and what is to come in the future. On the other hand, we
have Zoroastrianism, Christianity, Islam and Bahaism—
all strongly monotheistic faiths which speak of this Earth
as being momentary, the life to come being the focus of
their teachings. And last, but by no means the least, we
have Jainism which focuses on all three: the past, because
it believes in reincarnation; the present, because it believes
strongly in ahimsa or non-violence towards all living beings;
and the future which is future reincarnation, as well as
getting out of the cycle of birth and rebirth to regain the
soul's former status of complete bliss.

There are also completely different metaphysical points
of view in all these religions. In one model, you have a
Creator God who is beyond His creation and who has set

down for each soul an individual judgement at the end of this life. This will then either lead it up to heaven or consign it to hell for a temporary period. This is then followed by a cut-off day, referred to as Judgement Day, after which souls are resurrected here on Earth in which death and suffering disappear, and all created beings live in harmony forever with each other. This is the view of Zoroastrianism, Christianity and Islam. On the other hand, there is a completely different metaphysical point of view that has no God, no plan, but an endless cycle of birth, death and rebirth in which an individual's soul is trapped. The best that the soul can do is to get out of this trap and regain its original blissful spiritual existence. This is the Jain point of view.

In a third model, we have heaven and hell in the afterlife and reincarnation. This is the view of Hinduism in the Upanishads and in the Bhagavad Gita. Heaven and hell are temporary states of existence to which a soul is sent depending upon the law of karma, and it is upon exhaustion of the good or the evil that the soul has done that the soul then comes back to Earth and is reincarnated either in a happy or unhappy state, depending upon its residual karma. Jain and Buddhist thought doesn't exactly fit this model but also has, as part of the wheel of reincarnation, heavenly and hellish abodes in which the soul can transmigrate, and, depending upon the law of karma and the good or evil that it has done, move forward or backward in this wheel.

There is also have a fourth world view, which is to focus upon the present only, in which ethics play a most important part; and in this worldview you have Judaism and Sikhism, theistic religions, and Buddhism, Confucianism and Taoism, religions which are non-theistic, but which strongly emphasise virtuous living. Of course, Taoism's emphasis, apart from virtuous living, is how to blend with nature and not resist natural forces.

In a fifth world view, one encounters heaven and hell as also resurrection, all not to be taken literally. Heaven, hell and the resurrection are not places but states of mind, depending upon nearness or being far from Almighty God. This is the Baha'i worldview. Equally, in Confucianism and Taoism, heaven and hell are not to be taken literally. In Confucianism, heaven is a concept and hell does not exist, whereas in Taoism both heaven and hell are states of mind on which there is not much focus.

Heaven has different meanings in different world religions, just as hell also has different meanings. For example, in the Hindu religion, hell is referred to as *narak* which is Lord Yama's abode. The Bhagavatapurana tells us that this place is below the Earth, somewhere in the south, and it is Yama (who is also called Dharmaraja) who is the judge who lives in this abode. This abode is a temporary phase of existence of samsara, which as has been stated earlier, is the cycle of birth, rebirth and death. Chitragupta here maintains a record of the good and evil done by each soul, and evil is punished to the extent of the evil done.

There are as many as twenty-eight hells to which one is consigned depending upon what evil act has been performed.

Interestingly, Hinduism has no devil; it has worlds in which rakshasas and asuras, that is evil beings, reside, but no devil as the very embodiment of evil. As opposed to this, hell is the abode where Satan is sent by God in some of the theistic faiths. It is God, therefore, who controls hell and not Satan, Satan being a creation of God, a fallen angel. This is the Christian view of hell. On the other hand, in Islam, hell is a place where people burn, depending upon the deeds they have done. And Iblis is stated to be the devil. Iblis incidentally is not a fallen angel, but is a jinn or ghost, as in Islam, angels have no freedom of choice, whereas ghosts do. It is Iblis therefore, who was first consigned to hell as he refused to bow to God's greatest creation, the very first man, that is Adam.

In Zoroastrianism, in the Gathas, hell is considered to be a domain which is unreal. It is unreal because it is a place which will not exist forever, hell disappearing after Judgement Day. Equally in younger Zoroastrianism, hell is the abode of Ahriman who is, as we have seen earlier, a devil in the full-blown sense as being opposed to God in every way, who will ultimately be defeated. In Bahaism, hell again is not a place but is measured in terms of the distance that the soul is from God. In Taoism, there is a concept called *diyu,* where dead souls exist awaiting reincarnation, which again is very far from the kind of hell we have seen in theistic religions. Among the Jews, there is no devil and no hell, except in the Book of Enoch, today excluded from the Jewish canon, as borrowings from Zoroastrianism.

Conversely, heaven means different things in the different religions which speak of it. In the Rigveda, heaven is described as *svarga*, a place in which the gods reside and in which there is much merriment and music. In Zoroastrianism, heaven is spoken of as being the abode of song in which God and His angels reside and to which each individual soul goes before Judgement Day and the resurrection. In Judaism, heaven is the place where God and His angels reside, but man never goes there. The only exception is Prophet Elijah, who is stated in the Old Testament to be carried up to heaven upon his death. Unlike the other temporary abode of human beings in heaven in the other theistic religions, in Judaism, this is a permanent abode of God and His angels. In Bahaism, another theistic religion, heaven is measured as being close to God, and is a mental state and not an abode. Sikhism does not focus upon heaven and hell, except to say that these are mental states here on Earth itself. In Christianity and Islam, heaven is somewhat like the Zoroastrian heaven in which happiness reigns. It is the abode of God and His angels, an abode to which man goes temporarily, dependent upon the good deeds he has done here in this life, until Judgement Day. In Jainism and Buddhism, heaven is nothing but a place where celestial beings reside and which are part of the cycle of transmigration into which and out of which human beings go and return to Earth. Likewise, in Confucianism, as we have discussed earlier, heaven is a concept just as it is in Taoism.

Given these bewildering differences, is there anything that is common to all these world religions, and can we learn something new from each of them? It is important to understand what each world religion teaches us and then to follow and put into practice these teachings. In Hinduism, as has been expounded by the Bhagavad Gita, there are the three paths of salvation which lead to moksha. The third path, or the path of karma yoga or doing one's duty without the expectation of reward and renouncing the reward given, is the path that is strongly advocated for most human beings. There is also the differentiation between three gunas which are important to keep in mind when one acts in the world. Every act, therefore, can be sattvic or pure and good, rajasic or passionate, and therefore not good, or tamasic that is dark or ignorant. When one keeps these three gunas in mind and then performs every action, there is a constant reminder to stick to the path of virtue.

When we come to Zoroastrianism, the holy triad of good thoughts, good words and good deeds, which is the path of truth leading to God, is an excellent ethical way in which to conduct oneself, having God as the goal to be reached. In Judaism, we have life on Earth to be lived morally in accordance with Moses's Ten Commandments and in accordance with the laws laid down in the Book of Leviticus. The importance of Judaism is to be able to worship one God through obeying His commandments.

From Christianity, we learn how to love each other and to reach our Father who is in heaven owing to grace, the central belief being that the great Prophet Jesus came to Earth to intercede on our behalf with the Almighty and remit our sins so that we may reach God. The summation of the entire law into two is worthy of emulation: 'Love thy God with all thy heart and soul' and 'Treat thy neighbour as thyself'.

Islam teaches us to surrender to the will of Almighty God. We are told that if God wills something, nothing can stand in the way, and if God does not will something, nothing can be achieved. This religion teaches us that faith in God, good works and belief in the judgement of God will ultimately lead us to God. The religion of the Sikhs teaches us the importance of God's name and how to serve humanity in God's name. The concepts of *langar,* which is the mass feeding, free of charge, of anybody who comes to them, and *kar seva,* which is doing any task, howsoever menial, by a Sikh, howsoever highly placed, are two great pointers as to how to serve humanity in the name of God. The Bahai religion tells us how to remember God at all times and to strive only to reach God, as nearness to God is the single-most important thing that one can achieve both on Earth and in the afterlife.

Jainism teaches us the cardinal principle of ahimsa, which is non-violence to all living beings. It is one of the few religions which focuses on all living beings and not merely on mankind. The importance of ahimsa as a principle in a world that is full of war and strife cannot be overemphasized. Buddhism teaches us to recognize suffering as greed or desire beyond one's needs, and the importance of living morally, following the Eightfold path on this Earth. It also teaches us not to speculate on an afterlife which, according to it, is wholly unnecessary in dealing with suffering and its alleviation. Confucianism teaches us how to live life like a 'superior man', how to live by virtue alone, with filial and family devotion as its basis. Taoism teaches us to live life in accordance with nature and how not to resist nature, as resistance produces suffering.

In the end, therefore, we come back to the question: What is the commonality of all these great world faiths? One is the quest for becoming immortal, the cessation of death being central to human existence. Immortality in Buddhism, at least, is equated with release, but otherwise, in the other world religions, is an everlasting life of every soul either as a soul by itself or by merger with the Infinite in perfect bliss, in which all duality and all suffering disappears. The other great thing which world religions teach us is: 'As you sow, so shall you reap.' This again is a common bottomline with all the world faiths. There are, of course, exceptions in that one can attain God in Hinduism and Christianity through grace. Also, there are exceptions in Hindu strains of thought which are no longer extant today, like the Charvaka School and the Ajivika School where this principle does not obtain. By and large, it is this restraining principle which is of extreme importance in realizing that good begets good and that evil begets evil and recoils on the perpetrator.

The importance of understanding one's own religion and each other's religions and to practise what is good from all of them is the only way to live amicably and peaceably with each other, in the realization that all human beings are essentially the same, who custom and religion have divided. When this realization dawns on mankind, violence and misery give way to peace and happiness, as knowledge and wisdom replace ignorance and love replaces hatred. World wars give way to world peace so that happiness for all mankind gets finally achieved.

Acknowledgements

The author wishes to thank Miss Mayukhi Ghosh for the secretarial assistance rendered in writing this book.

Bibliography

A. Sacred Books of the East

Beal, Samuel. *The Fo-Sho-Hing-Tsan-King*. New Delhi: Atlantic Publishers and Distributors.

Bloomfield, M. *Hymns of the Atharva-Veda*. New Delhi: Atlantic Publishers and Distributors.

Buhler, G. *The Laws of Manu*. New Delhi: Ahuja Book Company.

Buhler, G. *The Sacred Laws of the Aryans*. Part I. New Delhi: Atlantic Publishers and Distributors.

Buhler, G. *The Sacred Laws of the Aryans*. Part II. New Delhi: Ahuja Book Company.

Cowell, E.B., F. Max Muller and J. Takakusu. *Buddhist Mahayana Texts*. New Delhi: Atlantic Publishers and Distributors.

Eggeling, J. *The Satapatha Brahmana*. 5 Parts. New Delhi: Atlantic Publishers and Distributors.

Jolly, Julius. *The Minor Law Books*. New Delhi: Atlantic Publishers and Distributors.

Kern, H. *The Saddharma-Pundarika*. New Delhi: Atlantic Publishers and Distributors.

Max Muller, F. *The Upanishads*. Parts 1, 2 & 3. New Delhi: Atlantic Publishers and Distributors.

Max Muller, F. *The Dharmmapada*. New Delhi: Atlantic Publishers and Distributors.

Max Muller, F., and H. Oldenberg. *The Grihya-Sutras*, Parts 1 & 2. New Delhi: Atlantic Publishers and Distributors.

Max Muller, F., and H. Oldenberg. *Vedic Hymns*. Parts 1–3. New Delhi: Atlantic Publishers and Distributors.

Palmer, E.H. *The Quran*. Part 1 & 2. New Delhi: Atlantic Publishers and Distributors.

Rhys Davids, T.W. *The Questions of King Milinda*. Part 1 & 2. New Delhi: Atlantic Publishers and Distributors.

Rhys Davids, T.W., and Hermann Oldenberg. *Vinaya Texts*. Parts 1–3. New Delhi: Atlantic Publishers and Distributors.

Rhys Davids, T.W. *Buddhist Sutras*. New Delhi: Atlantic Publishers and Distributors.

Rhys Davids, T.W. *Dialogues of the Buddha*. Vol. 1. Delhi: Low Price Publications, 1899.

Rhys Davids, T.W., and C.A.F. Rhys Davids. *Dialogues of the Buddha*. Vol. 2 & 3. Delhi: Low Price Publications, 1899.

Stone, Julius. *The Institutes of Visnu*. New Delhi: Atlantic Publishers and Distributors, 1880.

Telang, K.T. *The Bhagavadgita*. New Delhi: Atlantic Publishers and Distributors.

Thibaut, G. *The Vedanta Sutras.* Part 1–3. New Delhi: Atlantic Publishers and Distributors.

Winternitz, M. *A General Index of the Sacred Books of the East.* New Delhi: Atlantic Publishers and Distributors.

B. Hinduism

Abhedananda, Swami. *Reincarnation.* Calcutta: Ramakrishna Vedanta Math.

Abhedananda, Swami. *The Great Savior of the World.* Madras: Ramakrishna Vedanta Math, 1957.

Adi Sankaracarya's Dhanyastakam. Commentary by Swami Tejomayananda. Bombay: Central Chinmaya Mission Trust, 2001.

Adidevananda, Svami, trans. *Sri Ramanuja Gita Bhasya.* Madras: Sri Ramakrishna Math, 2022.

Alva, Joachim. *Men and Supermen of Hindustan.* Bombay: Thacker and Co. Ltd, 1943.

Astavakra Gita: Song of Self-realisation. Commentary by: Swami Chinmayananda. Mumbai: Central Chinmaya Mission Trust, 2018.

Aurobindo, Sri. *Letters on Yoga.* Vol. 2. Pondicherry: India Books, 1971.

Bose, D.N., and Hiralal Haldar. *Tantras: Their Philosophy and Occult Secrets.* Kolkata: Firma KLM Private Ltd, 1981.

Bose, Ram Chandra. *Hindu Philosophy: The Orthodox Systems.* New Delhi: Asian Educational Services, 1986.

Brahma Sutras. Delhi: Advaita Ashram.

Brent, Peter. *Godmen of India*. London: Penguin Books, 1972.

Brooke, Tal. *Sai Baba: Lord of the Air*. Vikas Publishing House Pvt. Ltd, 1979.

Candrasekharendra, Jagadguru Sri. *Ādi Sankara: His Life and Times.* Bombay: Bharatiya Vidya Bhavan, 2013.

Catuhsloki-Bhagavata. Mumbai: Central Chinmaya Mission Trust.

Chakraborti, Madhavadasa. *A Short History of Sanskrit Literature.* Delhi: Asian Publication Services, 1978.

Chandogya Upanisad: With Commentary of Sankaracarya. Translated by Swami Gambhirananda. Delhi: Advaita Ashram, 1983.

Chaudhuri, Asim. *Swami Vivekananda in Chicago*. West Bengal: Ramakrishna Mission,

Chidananda, Swami. *Mukunda Mala*. Mumbai: Central Chinmaya Mission Trust, 2013.

Chinmayananda, Swami. *The Holy Geeta*. Central Chinmaya Mission, Central Chinmaya Mission Trust, 1991.

———*Aadi Sankaracharya's Bhaja Govindam*. Mumbai: Central Chinmaya Mission Trust, 2020.

———*Atma–Bodha of Sri Adi Sankaracarya*. Mumbai: Central Chinmaya Mission Trust, 2012.

———*Bhaja Govindam*. Mumbai: Central Chinmaya Mission Trust, 2018.

———*Narada Bhakti Sutra*. Mumbai: Central Chinmaya Mission Trust, 2013.

———*Talks on Sankara's Vivekachoodamani*. Mumbai: Central Chinmaya Mission Trust, 1970.

Dasgupta, S.N. *A History of Sanskrit Literature*. Vol. 1. Calcutta: University of Calcutta, 1962.

Dilwali, Ashok. *Sayings from the Upanishads*. New Delhi: Niyogi Books, 2012.

———*Sayings from the Vedas*. New Delhi: Niyogi Books, 2006.

Doniger, Wendy. *The Hindus*. New Delhi: Penguin Viking, 2009.

Egenes, Thomas. *Introduction to Sanskrit*. Part 1. New Delhi: Motilal Banarsidass Publishers Private Limited, 1996.

Elst, Koenraad. *Who Is a Hindu? Hindu Revivalist Views of Animism, Buddhism, Sikhism and Other Offshoots of Hinduism*. New Delhi: Voice of India, 2002.

Ernest Hume, Robert. *The Thirteen Principal Upanishads: Translated from the Sanskrit: With an Outline of the Philosophy of the Upanishads*. 2nd ed. Oxford: Oxford University Press, 1996.

Gambhirananda, Swami, trans. *Brahma Sutra Bhasya of Shankaracharya*. Delhi: Advaita Ashram, 2000.

Glory of Krishna. Bombay: Central Chinmaya Mission Trust, 1983.

Gopalacharya, Mahuli R. *The Heart of the Rigveda*. Mumbai: Somaiya Publications, 1971.

Griffith, Ralph T.H. *The Hymns of Rigveda*. New Delhi: Motilal Banarsidass Publishers, 2017.

———*The Hymns of the Rgveda*. Vol. 2. Chaukhamba Amarabharati Prakashan, 2004.

Gupta, Shakti M. *Loves of Hindu Gods and Sages.* Mumbai: Allied Publishers, 1973.

———*Vishnu and His Incarnations.* Mumbai: Somaiya Publications Pvt. Ltd, 2006.

———*The Gospel of Sri Ramakrishna.* 3d ed. Madras: Sri Ramakrishna Math Chennai, 2013.

Hanson, V., Stewart, R., and Nicholson, S., eds. *Karma: Rhythmic Return to Harmony.* Delhi: Motilal Banarsidass Publishers Pvt. Ltd,

Hardo, Trutz. *True Cases of Children Who Have Lived before Reincarnation.* Mumbai: Jaico Publishing House, 2003.

Heehs, Peter. *Sri Aurobindo: A Brief Biography.* Oxford: Oxford University Press.

Herman, Arthur L. *The Problem of Evil and Indian Thought.* Delhi: Motilal Banarsidass Publishers Private Limited, 1993.

Hindu Scriptures, Ed. R.C. Zaehner. London: Everyman's Library, 1992.

Hymn to Sri Daksinamurti of Adi Sankaracarya, Commentary by: Swami Chinmayananda. Mumbai: Central Chinmaya Mission Trust, 2018.

Isherwood, Christopher. *Ramakrishna and His Disciples.* Delhi: Advaita Ashrama, 2002.

Iyengar, T.R.R. *Dictionary of Hindu Gods and Goddesses.* New Delhi: D.K. Printworld (P) Ltd, 2004.

Iyer, Kolar Krishna, and Chikkerur Dheerendra Acharya. *The Great Men and Women of Puranas.* New Delhi: Munshiram Manoharlal Publishers Pvt. Ltd, 2003.

Jagadananda, Swami. *Upadesa Sahasri of Sri Sankaracarya.* Madras: Shri Ramakrishna Math, 2023.

Kapur, R.L. *Another Way to Live: A Psychiatrist among Indian Ascetics.* Penguin Viking.

Keith, Berriedale. *Classical Sanskrit Literature.* Y.M.C.A. Publishing House, 1958.

Keshavadas, Sadguru Sant. *Gāyatrī: The Highest Meditation.* Delhi: Motilal Banarsidass Publications Pvt. Ltd, 1990.

Knappert, Jan. *Indian Mythology: An Encyclopedia of Myth and Legend.* HarperCollins Publishers, India, 1992.

Krishnamani, M.N. *Aadi Shankara's Bhajagovindam.* New Delhi: Rashtriya Sanskrit Sansthan, 1996.

Krishnamani, M.N. Shankara: *The Revolutionary.* New Delhi: Rajan Publications, 2001.

Lahari, Saundarya. *The Ocean of Beauty.* Chennai: Theosophical Publishing House, 2000.

Life of Sri Ramakrishna: Compiled from Various Authentic Sources. Advaita Ashrama.

Madhavananda, Swami. *Vivekachudamani of Sri Sankaracharya.* Madras: Sri Ramakrishna Math.

———*Uddhava Gita: The Last Message of Shri Krishna.* Delhi: Advaita Ashram, 1971.

Mahadevan, T.M.P. *Ramana Maharshi: The Sage of Arunācala.* Vikas Publishing House Pvt. Ltd, 1977.

Mahadevan, T.M.P., trans. *Sarasvati: Sri Sankaracarya of Kanci Kamakoti Pitha.* Bombay: Bharatiya Vidya Bhavan.

Monier-Williams, Monier. *Hinduism and its Sources.* New Delhi: Munshiram Manoharlal Publishers, 2003.

Moor, Edward. *The Hindu Pantheon.* New Delhi: Asian Educational Services, 1999.

Mueller, F. Max, trans. *The Upanisads.* Part 1 & 2. New York: Dover Publications, 1962.

Nanda, Swami Ramakrishna. *Life of Sri Ramanuja.* Madras: Sri Ramakrishna Math, 1985.

Navajata. *Sri Aurobindo.* New Delhi: National Book Trust, 2000.

Nikhilananda, Swami. *Life of Sri Ramakrishna.* Foreword by Mahatma Gandhi. Delhi: Advaita Ashram, 1928.

Nikhilananda, Swami., trans. *Self-Knowledge: Sri Sankaracarya.* Madras: Sri Ramakrishna Math, 1947.

Oman, John Campbell. *The Mystics, Ascetics, and Saints of India.* London: T. Fisher Unwin, 1903.

Pancikaranam of Sri Sankaracarya. Delhi: Advaita Ashram, 2022.

Pande, Govind Chandra. *Life and Thought of Sankaracarya.* Delhi: Motilal Banarsidass Publishers Pvt. Ltd, 1998.

Pillai, R.N. *Veerabrahmam: India's Nostradamus Saint.* New Delhi: Abhinav Publications, 1991.

Prabhavananda, Swami. *Patanjali Yoga Sutras.* Madras: Sri Ramakrishna Math, 2008.

Radhakrishnan, *Bhagavadgita.* Mumbai: Blackie & Son (India) Ltd, 1977.

Radhakrishnan, S. *Bhagavad Gita.* London: George Allen and Unwin Ltd, 1970.

———*Brahma Sutra*. London: George Allen and Unwin Ltd.

———*The Principal Upanisads*. New Delhi: HarperCollins Publishers India, 2010.

Raghavachar, S.S. *Ramanuja on the Gita*. Delhi: Advaita Ashram, 2022.

Rajachandra, Srimad. *The Self-Realization: Translation of Atma-Siddhi*.

Rajagopalachari, C. *Mahabharata*. 47th ed. Mumbai: Bhavan's Book University, 1951.

Rajaram, Navaratna S. *Nationalism and Distortions of Indian History*. 2nd ed. Bangalore: Naimisha Research Foundation, 2002.

Ranganathananda, Swami. *The Approach to Truth in Vedanta*. Delhi: Advaita Ashram, 2022.

Reminiscences of Swami Vivekananda: His Eastern and Western Admirers. Delhi: Advaita Ashrama, 2017.

Renou, Louis, *Hinduism*. London: Prentice-Hall International, 1961.

Sadhana Panchakam by Adi Sankara (with commentary from Swami Chinmayananda). Chinmaya Prakashan, Central Chinmaya Mission Trust, 2018.

Sankara: The Missionary. Chinmaya Prakashan, 2018.

Sankaracarya, Sri Adi. *Aparoksanubhuti: Intimate Experience of the Reality* (Commentary by Swami Chinmayananda). Mumbai: Central Chinmaya Mission Trust, 2015.

Sankaracarya, Sri Adi. *Tattvabodhah*. Commentary by Swami Tejomayananda. Mumbai: Central Chinmaya Mission Trust, 2009.

Sankaracarya. *Eight Upanisads*. Vols 1 & 2. Translated by Swami Gambhirananda. Delhi: Advaita Ashram, 2001.

Sankaracarya. *Svetasvatara Upanisad*. Translated by Swami Gambhirananda. Delhi: Advaita Ashram, 1986.

Sankaracarya. *The Brhandaranyaka Upanisad*. Translated by Swami Madhavananda. Delhi: Advaita Ashrama, 2021.

Sankaracharya. *Tattva Bodha*. Mumbai: Central Chinmaya Mission Trust, 1981.

Saraswati, Swami Dayanand. *Light of Truth*. New Delhi: Sarvadeshik Arya Pratinidhi Sabha, 1984.

Saraswati, Swami Prakashanand. *The True History and the Religion of India: A Concise Encyclopaedia of Authentic Hinduism*. New Delhi: Motilal Banarsidass Publishers, 2002.

Sastry, T.S. Narayana. *The Age of Sankara*. Kolkata: B.G. Paul & Co., 1916.

Satguru, Sivaya. *Tirukural: Ethical Masterpiece of the Tamil People*. New Delhi: Abhinav Publications, 2000.

Saundarya Lahari: Inundation of Divine Splendour of Sri Sankaracarya. (Transliteration, Translation and Commentary by Swami Tapasyananda). Madras: Sri Ramakrishna Math, 2020.

Selections from Swami Vivekananda. Delhi: Advaita Ashram, 2001.

Sen, K.M. *Hinduism*. Gurugram: Penguin Random House: 2020.

Shelat, Kirit N. *Yug Purush: Pujya Pramukh Swami Maharaj*. Ahmedabad: Shri Bhagwati Trust.

Shourie, Arun. *Hinduism: Essence and Consequence.* Vikas Publishing House Pvt. Ltd, 1979.

Sidharth, B. G. *The Celestial Key to the Vedas: Discovering the Origins of the Worlds's Oldest Civilisation.* Rochester: Inner Traditions International, 2000.

Sri Adi Sankara's Vakya Vritti: Exhaustive Analysis of That Thou Art. Commentary by Swami Chinmayananda. Bombay: Central Chinmaya Mission Trust, 2014.

Sri Sankaracarya's Laghu Vakya Vrtti with Commentary. Delhi: Advaita Ashram, 2010.

Subramaniam, Kamala. *Srimad Bhagavatam* 8th ed. Mumbai: Bharatiya Vidya Bhavan, 2003.

Tagore. *Bhagavata Skanda and Garuda Puranas.* Delhi: Motilal Banarsidass.

Tapasyananda, Swami. *Sri Chaitanya Mahaprabhu: His Life, Religion and Philosophy.* Madras: Sri Ramakrishna Math, 2023.

Tapasyananda, Swami. *Sri Madhavacarya: His Life, Religion and Philosophy.* Madras: Sri Ramakrishna Math, 2012.

———*Sri Nimbarka: His Life, Religion and Philosophy.* Madras: Sri Ramakrishna Math, 2009.

———*Sri Vallabhacarya: His Life, Religion and Philosophy.* Madras: Sri Ramakrishna Math, 2004.

Tathagatananda, Swami. *Glimpses of Great Lives.* New York: The Vedanta Society of New York.

Tejomayananda, Swami. *Bhakti Sudha.* Mumbai: Central Chinmaya Mission Trust, 2019.

———Tejomayananda, Swami. *Sri Kapila Gita*. Mumbai: Central Chinmaya Mission Trust, 2015.

———Tejomayananda, Swami. *Upadesa Sara*. Mumbai: Central Chinmaya Mission Trust, 2010.

———Tejomayananda, Swami. *Yoga Vasistha Sara Sangrahah*. Mumbai: Central Chinmaya Mission Trust, 2004.

The Bhagavad Gita. Translated by Laurie L. Patton. London: Penguin Classics, 2008.

The Life of Swami Vivekananda: His Eastern and Western Disciples. Delhi: Advaita Ashrama, 2009.

*The Second Krishnamurti Read*er. Ed. Mary Lutyens. London: Penguin Books, 2002.

Vasu, Rai Bahadur Srisa Chandra, trans. *The Vedanta-Sutras of Badarayana: with the Commentary of Baladeva*. New Delhi: Oriental Books Reprint Corporation.

Verma, Justice J.S. Iqbal, A. Ansari, B.I. Laskar, Abu Hakim, and Ahmad Rashid Shervani. *Alpjan: A Chronicle of Minorities,* Vol. 3, Social Advancement and Development Trust.

Vimalananda, Swamini, trans. *Drg Drisya Viveka, Commentary by Swami Tejomayananda*. Mumbai: Central Chinmaya Mission Trust, 2018.

Vivekjivandas, Sadhu. *Hinduism: An Introduction*. Parts 1 & 2. Gujarat: Swaminarayan Aksharpith, 2011.

Warrier, A.G. Krishna. *God in Advaita*. Shimla: Indian Institute of Advanced Study, 1977.

Weiss, Dr Brian. *Many Lives, Many Masters*. UK: Piatkuss, 1994.

Williams, M. Monier. *Hinduism.* Kolkata: Susil Gupta (India) Ltd, 1951.

Yogananda, Sri Sri Paramahansa. *God Talks with Arjuna: The Bhagavad Gita, Part 1 and 2.* West Bengal: Yogoda Satsanga Society of India, 2009.

Zaehner, R.C. *Hindu Scriptures.* Rupa & Co.,1995.

Zaehner, R.C. *Hinduism (Opus).*

Zaehner, R.C. *Hinduism.* Oxford: Oxford University Press, 1966.

Zaehner, R.C. *The Bhagavad-Gita: With a Commentary Based on the Original Sources.* Oxford: Oxford University Press.

Zaehner, R.C., trans. *Hindu Scriptures.* London: J.M. Dent & Sons Ltd, 1938.

C. Zoroastrianism

Anklesaria, Behramgore T. *Pahlavi Vendidad.* Mumbai: The K.R. Cama Oriental Institute.

Boyce, Mary. *Textual Sources for the Study of Zoroastrianism.* Chicago: The University of Chicago Press & the University of Manchester Press, 1990.

Cairae, Harsh Mahaan. *An Aryan Journey.* New Delhi: Rupa Publications, 2014.

Chatterji, Jatindra Mohan. *The Hymns of Atharvan Zarathushtra.* The Parsi Zoroastrian Association.

Daryaee, Touraj. *Sasanian Persia: The rise and fall of an empire.* London: I.B. Tauris & Co. Ltd.

Dhalla, Maneckji Nusservanji. *History of Zoroastrianism*. Mumbai: The K.R. Cama Oriental Institute, 1963.

Dhalla, Maneckji Nusservanji. *Zoroastrian Theology*. Kessinger Publishing, 2011.

Dharmesteter, J., and H.L. Mills. *The Zend-Avesta, Part-I: The Vendidas*. Delhi: Atlantic Publishers and Distributors.

Dharmesteter, J., and H.L. Mills. *The Zend-Avesta, Part-II: The Sirozahs, Yasts and Nyayis*. New Delhi: Atlantic Publishers and Distributors.

Dharmesteter, J., and H.L. Mills. *The Zend-Avesta, Part-III: The Yasna*. New Delhi: Atlantic Publishers and Distributors.

Duchesne-Guillemin, J. *Religion of Ancient Iran*. Linden House, 1910.

Finkel, Irving, ed. *The Cyrus Cylinder: The King of Persia's Proclamation from Ancient Babylon*. London: I.B. Tauris & Co., 2013.

Gershevitch, Ilya. *The Avestan Hymn to Mithra: With an Introduction*. Cambridge: Cambridge University Press, 2008.

Haug, Martin. *The Parsis: Essays on their Sacred Language, Writings and Religion*. New Delhi: Cosmo Publications, 1907.

Hinnells, John R. *Zoroastrianism and the Parsis: Selected Works of John R. Hinnells*. 1st ed. Routledge, 2018.

Jackson, A.V. Williams. *Zoroastrian Studies*. Vol. 12. Columbia: Columbia University Indo-Iranian Series.

Kanga, Prof. Ervad Maneck Furdoonji. *Yasht-Ba-Maani*. Bombay: The Trustees of the Parsi Punchayat Funds and Properties.

Kriwaczek, Paul. *In Search of Zarathustra: The First Prophet and the Ideals That Changed the World*. Knopf, 2003.

Llewellyn-Jones, Lloyd. *Persians: The Age of the Great Kings*. New York: Basic Books, 2022.

Menant, Delphine. *The Parsis, Volume III*. Danai.

Murzban, M.M. *The Parsis*.Vol. 1 & 2. Danai.

Sethna, Tehmurasp Rustamji. *Yashts in Roman Script with Translation*. T.R. Sethna, 1976.

Taraporewala, Dr Irach J.S. *The Divine Songs of Zarathushtr*. Bombay: Hukhta Foundation, 1967.

———*Zoroastrian Morals*. B.I. Taraporewala.

———*Zoroastrianism*. B.I. Taraporewala.

West, E.W. *Pahlavi Texts*. Parts 1–5. New Delhi: Atlantic Publishers and Distributors.

West, M. *The Hymns of Zoroaster: A new translation of the most ancient sacred texts of Iran*. London: I. B. Tauris & Co. Ltd.

Wilson, John. *The Parsi Religion*. Indigo Books, 2005.

———*The Parsi Religion*. Toronto: Indigo Books, 2003.

Zaehner, R.C. *The Dawn and Twilight of Zoroastrianism*. Weidenfeld and Nicolson, 1961.

———*Zurvan: A Zoroastrian Dilemma*. Oxford: Oxford at the Clarendon Press.

D. Buddhism

Armstrong, Karen. *Buddha*. Phoenix, 2006.

Bahm, A.J. *Philosophy of the Buddha*. Vikas Publishing House, 1982.

Bapat, Prof. P.V., ed. *2500 Years of Buddhism*. Publications Division, Ministry of Information and Broadcasting, Government of India, 2023.

Carus, Paul. *Buddha, the Gospel*. Chicago: The Open Court Publishing Company, 1894.

Chinmayananda, Swami. *Tune in the Mind (Japa Gayatri)*. Mumbai: Central Chinmaya Mission Trust, 2018.

Conze, Edward, trans. *Buddhist Scriptures*. Penguin Books, 1959.

Conze, Edward. *A Short History of Buddhism*. Mandala Books, 1980.

David-Neel, Alexandra. *Buddhism: Its Doctrines and Its Methods*. Universal, 1978. Diwakar, R.R. *Bhagwan Buddha*. Bombay: Bharatiya Vidya Bhavan, 1960.

Dutt, Nalinaksha. *Buddhist Sects in India*. Calcutta Oriental Press, 1998.

Elenjimittam, Anthony. *The Dhammapada*. Ugo Mursia Editore, 2019.

Evans-Wentz, W.Y. *The Tibetan Book of the Dead*. Oxford: Oxford University Press, 1957.

Feer, M.L. *A Study of the Jātakas*. Kolkata: Susil Gupta (India) Private Ltd, 1875.

Gotama the Buddha: His Life and His Teaching. Vipassana Research Institute, 1988.

Horner, I.B. *Women under Primitive Buddhism*. Delhi: Motilal Banarsidass, 1930.

Humphreys, Christmas, ed. *The Wisdom of Buddhism.* Oxford and Ibh Publishing Co., 1960.

Humphreys, Christmas. *Buddhism.* London: Penguin Books, 1951.

———*Buddhism.* Penguin Books, 1951.

Kapleau, Roshi Philip. *The Three Pillars of Zen: Teaching, Practice and Enlightenment.* Anchor Books, 1989.

Lama, Dalai. *Ancient Wisdom, Modern World: Ethics for the New Millennium.* Abacus, 1999.

Lee, Jung Young. *Death and Beyond in the Eastern Perspective.* Interface book, 1974.

Ling, Trevor, ed. *The Buddha's Philosophy of Man: Early Buddhist Dialogues.* Dent, 1981.

Ling, Trevor. *The Buddha: Buddhist Civilization in India and Ceylon.* Penguin Books, 1973.

Mullin, Glenn H. *The Fourteen Dalai Lamas.* Jaico Publishing House, 2008.

Oldenberg, Hermann. *Buddha: His Life, His Doctrine, His Order.* Aravali Books, 1997.

Price, A.F., and Wong Mou-Lam., trans. *The Diamond Sutra and The Sutra of Hui Neng.* Shambhala Publications, 2005.

Radhakrishnan. *Dhammapada.* Oxford: Oxford University Press, 1997.

Rahula, Walpola Sri. *What the Buddha Taught.* Rev. ed. New York: Grove Press Inc., 1959.

Robinson, Richard H. *The Buddhist Religion: A Historical Introduction*. Dickenson Publishing Company, Inc., 1970.

Rockhill, W. Woodville, trans. *The Life of the Buddha and the Early History of His Order*. Orientalia Indica Publishers, 2007.

Saddhaloka. *Encounters with Enlightenment: Stories from the Life of the Buddha*. New Delhi: Wisdom Tree, 2008.

Schumann, H.W. *The Historical Buddha*. Arkana, 1989.

Suzuki, D.T. *An Introduction to Zen Buddhism*. Rider, 1934.

Suzuki, D.T. *Essays in Zen Buddhism: First Series*. Rider and Company, 1927.

Taimni, I.K. *The Science of Yoga*. Chennai: The Theosophical Publishing House, 2018.

Tandon, S.N. *A Re-Appraisal of Patanjali's Yoga-Sutras: In the Light of Buddha's Teaching*. Vipassana Research Institute, 1995.

Thakur, Amarnath. *Buddha and Buddhist Synods in India and Abroad*. Abhinav Publications, 1996.

Thera, Narada Maha. *The Dhammapada*. Maha Bodhi Society of India,

Tiyavanich, Kamala. *Sons of the Buddha*. Delhi: Wisdom Publications, 2007.

Trainor, Kevin. *Buddhism*. London: Duncan Baird Publishers, 2001.

Watts, Alan W. *The Way of Zen*. Pelican Book, 1962.

World of the Buddha: An Introduction to Buddhist Literature. Edited with Introduction and Commentaries by Licien Stryk. New York: Grove Press, Inc., 2007.

E. Sikhism

Singh, Bhagat, and G.P. Singh, trans. *Japji: The Morning Prayer*. Hemkunt.

Duggal, Kartar Singh. *The Prescribed Sikh Prayers*. New Delhi: Abhinav Publications, 1980.

Doabia, Harbans Singh. *Guru Tegh Bahadar Ji (Life History, Sacred Hymns & Teachings) (revised by Justice Tejinder Singh Doabia (Retd)*. Doabia Foundation, 1975.

Cunningham, J.D. *History of the Sikhs*. Edited by HLO Garrett. Low Price Publications, 1849.

Cole, Owen. *The Place of the Ten Gurus in the Sikh Religion*. Rupa Paperback.

Grewal, J.S., and Irfan Habib, ed. *Sikh History from Persian Sources*. New Delhi: Tulika, 2001.

Cole, W. Owen, and Piara Singh Sambhi. *The Sikhs: Their Religious Beliefs and Practices*. Routledge, 1978.

Macauliffe, Max Arthur. *The Sikh Religion: Its Gurus, Sacred Writings and Authors*, Vol. 1 – 5. Oxford at the Clarendon Press,

F. Islam

Ahmad, Khurshid, ed. *Islam: Its Meaning and Message*. Islamic Council of Europe, 1975.

Ali, Maulana Muhammad. *The Holy Quran*. Ahmadiyya Anjuman Ishaat, 1996.

Arberry A.J. *Tales from the Masnavi*. George Allen & Unwin Ltd, 1961.

Arberry, A.J. *Revelation and Reason in Islam*. George Allen & Unwin, 1957.

Arnold, Sir Thomas S. *Painting in Islam*. Oxford: Clarendon Press. 1928.

Brockelmann, Carl. *History of the Islamic Peoples*. Routledge & Kegan Paul, 1982.

Dibble, R.F. *Mohammed*. Hutchinson & Co. Ltd, 1926.

———*Mohammed*. London: Hutchinson & Co., 1930.

Eaton, Richard Maxwell. *Sufis of Bijapur, 1300–1700*. Princeton University Press, 1978.

Esposito, John L. *Islam: The Straight Path*. New York: Oxford University Press, 2006.

Gatje, Helmut. *The Quran and Its Exegesis*. Oxford: One World, 1996.

Glubb, Sir John. *The Life and Times of Muhammad*. NY: Stein & Day, 1971.

Guillaume, Alfred. *Islam*. Pelican Book, 1954.

Hamad, Abdul Wahid. *Companions of the Prophet* 1–3. M.E.L.S

Ibrahim, Sliman Ben, and E. Dinet. *The Life of Mohammad*. Studio Edition,1990.

Karen Armstrong. *Muhammad*. Victor Gollancz, 1992.

Pickthall, Md. Marmaduke. *The Meaning of the Glorious Qur'an*. Universal Books, 1998.

Pirenne, Henri. *Mohammed and Charlemagne.* George Allen & Unwin, 1937.

Rodinson, Maxime. *Mohammed.* Penguin Books, 1991.

Salahi, M.A. *Mohammed: Man and Prophet.* Element Books, 1995.

Shah, Idries. *The Sufis.* Anchor Books, 1971.

Sharif, Ja'far. *Islam in India.* Delhi: Oriental Books Reprint Corporation, 1972.

Stewart, Desmond. *Mecca.* New York: Newsweek, 1980.

Warraq, Ibn. *The Quest for the Historical Muhammad.* Prometheus Books, 2000.

Zakaria, Rafiq. *Muhammad and the Quran.* Penguin Books, 1992.

G. Jainism

Bhattacharya, N.N. *Jain Philosophy: Historical Outline.* Delhi: Munshiram Manoharlal Pvt. Ltd, 1976.

Chatterjee, Asim Kumar. *A Comprehensive History of Jainism.* Delhi: Munshiram Manoharlal Publishers Pvt. Ltd, 2000.

Dundas, Paul. *The Jains.* 2d ed. Routledge, 2002.

Glasenapp, Dr. Helmutu von. *The Doctrine of Karma in Jain Philosophy.* Bombay: The Trustees, Bai Vijbai Jivanlal Panalal Charity Fund, 1942.

Jacobi, Hermann. *Jaina Sutras* Part 1–2. New Delhi: Atlantic Publishers and Distributors, 1895.

Jain, C.R. *What Is Jainism (Essays and Addresses -1).* The Indian Press Ltd.

Jain, Jagdishchandra. *Life in Ancient India as Depicted in Jaina Canon and Commentaries.* Delhi: Munshiram Manoharlal Publishers Pvt. Ltd, 1984.

Kalghatgi, T.C. *Study of Jainism.* Jaipur: Prakrit Bharati Academy, 1988.

Kamkumarnandi, Upadhyaya. *Universal Message of Jainism.* 1997.

Kumar, Muni Shiv. *The Doctrine of Liberation in Indian Religion with Special reference to Jainism.* Delhi: Munshiram Manoharlal Pvt. Ltd, 2000.

Nahar, P.C., and K.C. Ghosh. *An Encyclopaedia of Jainism.* Sri Satguru Publications, 1971.

Parikh, Vastupal. *Jainism and the New Spirituality.* Toronto: Peace Publications, 2002.

Sanghvi, Shri Jayatilal S. *Treatise on Jainism.* Forgotten Books, 2008.

Singhvi, Dr L.M. *The Jain Declaration of Nature.* Mayer Printers Co., 1990.

Sircar, D.C., ed. *Religion and Culture of the Jains.* Calcutta: University of Calcutta, 1973.

Stevenson, Sinclair. *The Heart of Jainism.* Delhi: Munshiram Manoharlal Pvt. Ltd, 1915.

Studies in Jainism. Calcutta: The Ramkrishna Mission, Institute of Culture, 2002.

H. Christianity

Crosson, John. *The Historical Jesus.* Harper San Francisco, 1992.

Eusebius, *The History of the Church*. Penguin, 1989.

Johnson, Paul. *A History of Christianity*. Touchstone, 1995.

Laux, Rev. John. *Church History*. Benziger Brothers, 1937.

MacCulloch, Diarmaid. *A History of Christianity*. Allen Lane, 2009.

McGrath, Alister. *Christian Theology*. Blackwell, 1993.

McManners, John. *The Oxford History of Christianity*. Oxford: Oxford University Press, 1993.

Porter, J.R. *Jesus Christ: The Jesus of History*. Barnes & Noble Press, 2004.

Sanders, E.P. *The Historical Figure of Jesus*. Penguin, 1993.

Wills, Garry. *St. Augustine*. Weidenfeld & Nicolson, 1999.

Wilson, Ian. *Jesus: The Evidence*. Pan Books, 1964.

I. Judaism

Armstrong, Karen. *A History of God*. Ballantine Books, 1993.

Feiler, Bruce. *Abraham*. HarperCollins, 2002.

Franck, Adolphe. *The Kabbalah*. NY: Bell Publishing Co., 1940.

Johnson, Paul. *A History of the Jews*. Phoenix Giant, 1987.

Josephus. *Wars of the Jews*. Sacred Texts.

———*Antiquities of the Jews*. Sacred Texts.

Lancaster, Brian. *The Elements of Judaism*. Element, 1993.

Ouaknin, Marc-Alain. *Mysteries of the Kabbabh*. New York: Abbeville Press Publishers, 2000.

Rodkinson, Michael L. *The Babylonian* Talmud. Sacred Texts, 1918.

J. Bahaism

Bahaullah. *Ketab-i-Aqdas*. Bahai World Centre, 1992.

——*Ketab-i-Iqan*. US, 1989.

——*The Hidden Words of Bahaullah*. US, 1985.

——*The Proclamation of Bahaullah*. US, 1978.

——*Tablets of Bahaullah*. US, 1988.

——*Gleanings from the Writings of Bahaullah*. US, 1990.

K. Confucianism and Taoism

Alitto, Guy S. *The Last Confucian*. California: University of California Press, 1979.

Confucius, Arthur Waley, *The Analects of Confucius*. Psychology Press, 2005.

Rainey, Lee Dian. *Confucius and Confucianism: The Essentials*. Wiley-Blackwell, 2010.

Soothill, William Edward, trans. *The Analects or the Conversations of Confucius with His Disciples and Certain Others*. Oxford: Oxford University Press, 1951.

Tzu, Lao. *Tao te Ching*. London: Penguin Books, 2003.

Weber, Max. *The Religion of China: Confucianism and Taoism*. Glencoe, Illinois: The Free Press, 1951.

L. Philosophy

Atreya, B.L. *The Yogavasistha and Its Philosophy*. Darshana Printers, 1936.

Colebrooke, H.T. *Essays of the Religion and Philosophy of Hindus*. Ashok Publications, 2019.

Dasgupta, Surendranath. *A History of Indian Philosophy*. Vols. 1–5. Cambridge: Cambridge University Press.

Dubey, S.P. *Facets of Recent Indian Philosophy: Problems of Indian Philosophy*. Vol. 3. Indian Council of Philosophical Research, 1944.

Fraunwallner, Erich. *History of Indian Philosophy*. Vols. 1 & 2. Delhi: Motilal Banarsidass Publishers, 2008, 2023.

Muller, Friedrich Max. *The Six Systems of Indian Philosophy*. Chronicle Books, 1899.

Puligandla, R. *Fundamentals of Indian Philosophy*. Abingdon Press, 1975.

Radhakrishnan, S. *Indian Philosophy*. Vols. 1 & 2. George Allen & Unwin Ltd, 1923.

———*Contemporary Indian Philosophy*. Allen and Unwin Ltd,

Ramacharaka, Yogi. *The Philosophies and Religions of India*. L.N. Fowler & Co., 1909.

Ranganathan, Shyam. *Ethics and the History of Indian Philosophy*. Delhi: Motilal Banarsidass Publishers, 2007.

Zimmer, Heinrich. *Philosophies of India*. Revised ed. Princeton University Press, 1969.

M. Miscellaneous

Brunton, Paul. *A Search in Secret India*. Rider & Co., 2003.

Embree, Ainslie T., ed. *Sources of Indian Tradition*. 2 Vols. 2d ed. Columbia University Press, 1988.

Hay, Stephen. *Sources of Indian Tradition*. 2d ed, Vols. 1 & 2. Viking,

Mackenzie, Donald A. *India: Myths and Legends*. Scotland: Gresham Publishing Company, 1913.

Radhakrishnan, S. *Kalki or the Future of Civilization*. Jegan Paul, Trench Trubner and Co. Ltd, 1929.

———*East and West in Religion*. Allen and Unwin Ltd, 1933.

———*East and West: Some Reflections*. Allen and Unwin Ltd, 1955.

———*Eastern Religions and Western Thought*. Allen and Unwin Ltd, 1933.

———*Great Indians*. Allen and Unwin Ltd, 1923.

——— *Idealist View of Life*. Allen and Unwin Ltd, 1932.

———*India and China*. Allen and Unwin Ltd, 1944.

———*Is This Peace*? Allen and Unwin Ltd, 1973.

Singh, Khushwant. *We Indians*. New Delhi: Orient Paperbacks, a division of Vision Books Pvt. Ltd, 1982.

Voigt, Johannes H. *Max Mueller: The Man and His Ideas*. Firma, 1967.

Index

Scan QR code to access the
Penguin Random House India website